# Exploring the Quiet Lanes and Villages of West Dorset

# Exploring the Quiet Lanes and Villages of West Dorset

## Jackie Winter

Roving
Press

Published by Roving Press Ltd
4 Southover Cottages, Frampton, Dorset, DT2 9NQ, UK
Tel: 01300 321531
www.rovingpress.co.uk

Contents are believed to be correct at time of going to print. The publishers cannot
accept responsibility for errors or omissions, or for changes in details given. Every
effort has been made to check locations and ensure descriptions and directions
are correct. We welcome information from readers regarding changes to routes, to
keep the book up to date.

First published 2020 by Roving Press Ltd

ISBN: 978-1-906651-343

British Library Cataloguing in Publication Data
A catalogue record for this book is available from the British Library

Cover design by Tim Musk

Maps based on OpenStreet Map © OpenStreetMap contributors.

Set in 11.5/13 pt by Beamreach (www.beamreachuk.co.uk)
Printed and bound by Henry Ling Ltd., at the Dorset Press, Dorchester, DT1 1HD.

# Contents

*Rawlsbury Camp near Bulbarrow Hill.*

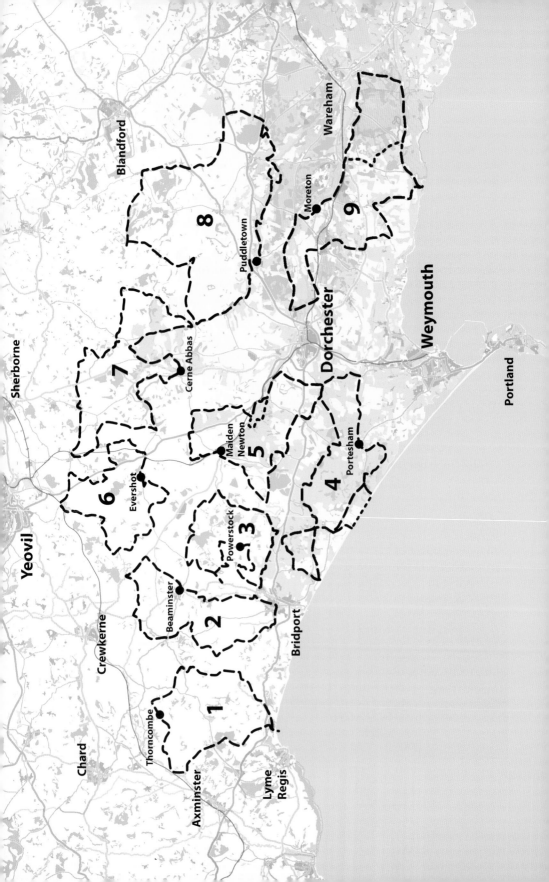

# Introduction

There's something endearing about a tandem. People like to stop and chat and everyone has a story to tell. When we go cycling, the tandem tends to look as if it's on a month's holiday, because we always take a front bag and panniers filled with waterproofs, spare jumpers, a picnic bag and two flasks of hot water. The flasks weigh a ton, but after they've provided elevenses, lunchtime drinks and afternoon tea, there's never any water left. It's an old-fashioned way to cycle. The youngsters don't seem to carry more than a water bottle, an energy bar, a pump and a spare inner tube.

Finding things by the side of the road often happens when we're cycling. A pair of sunglasses, an adjustable spanner and once a wallet stuffed full of money, which we were able to personally re-unite with its grateful owner. Back in the 1980s we were always finding abandoned lads' mags.

It's not unusual for passing motorists to shout 'Can you ride tandem?' This phrase originates from a 1970s' PG Tips advert in which it was used by a male chimp as a chat-up line. It's been hurled at us again and again over the years and tests our patience to the limits. Of course we can ride tandem! What else does it look like we're doing?

Tandems are very speedy on the descent and we frequently whizz downhill in excess of 40 mph. Uphill it's a different matter because tandems are slower than a solo bike. On uphill stretches Allan pushes the tandem while I follow at my own pace. This is one of the advantages of riding a tandem, along with having no responsibility for braking, steering or changing gear. As I've never learned to ride a bike I don't instinctively want to do any of those things and I'm perfectly happy pedalling along and enjoying the scenery, which is not totally obscured by my husband's backside, which is a popular misconception.

The routes in this book are all original and according to our tried and tested whim. Although they may encompass sections of the National Cycle Network (NCN) they do not follow them exactly. We frequently stop in village churchyards for elevenses or a picnic lunch. These are always peaceful places and generally have a seat, often with a view. Over the years, I became intrigued by the dedications on these seats and have discovered interesting life histories of much-loved local characters.

The book will certainly be of interest to cyclists, young and not so young, but it should also appeal to non-cyclists. Allan and I aren't concerned with how many miles we clock up. The ride itself and the places on route are of primary importance, so the book isn't intended for diehard cyclists who just want to burn up the miles. Many of the routes pass Dorset Wildlife Trust (DWT) nature reserves and places of antiquity, worth a pause. Moreover, readers who are curious about Dorset's past and its people, especially those who lived exceptional lives but who have often been almost forgotten, should find plenty of interest in this book.

Cyclists please be warned though – West Dorset is hilly! Rather than describing the gradients in detail for each route, we've highlighted the steeper and/or longer climbs in red on the Route Maps. We've also included red exclamation marks on the maps to highlight things like busier roads and junctions, and steep narrow descents such as those into Stoke Abbott (Route 2), Loscombe (Route 3) and Batcombe (Route 7).

We hope you enjoy this wonderful part of the county as much as we do.

*Ruscombe Lane between Powerstock and South Poorton.*

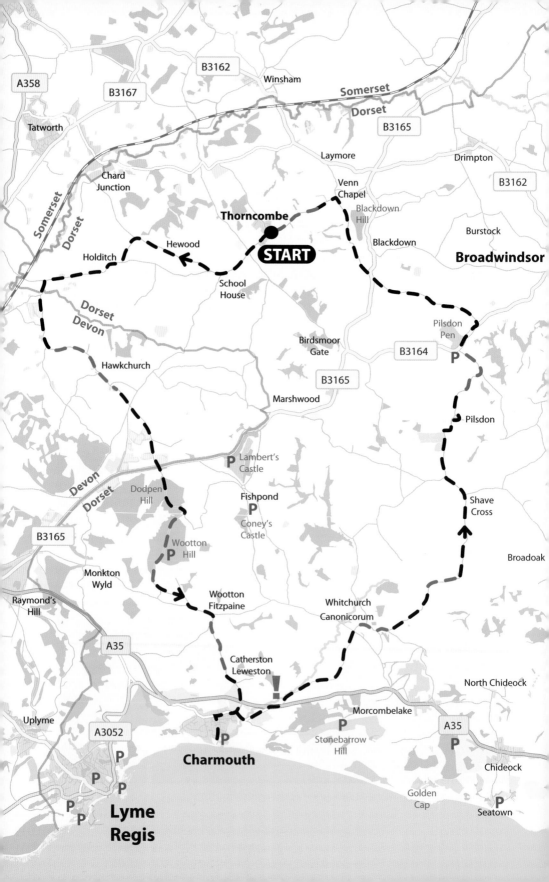

# Route 1 – Thorncombe

*(visiting Hawkchurch, Wootton Fitzpaine, Catherston Leweston, Charmouth, Whitchurch Canonicorum and Pilsdon)*

**Distance:** 24 miles (39 km)

**Hills:** 650 m elevation change, three significant hills

**OS map:** Explorer 116

**Brief description:** Passing through beech woods, popular with foragers, at the Jurassic coast we linger to enjoy the views. We pay our respects at a shrine to a local saint. Passing a Jacobean manor house, home to a community of people who help those in trouble, we are treated to views over the Marshwood Vale and of Dorset's highest hills.

From St Mary's Church (front entrance) we set off, passing Thorncombe Village Shop. This community-run shop has a popular café with outdoor seating, a favourite with cyclists and walkers, especially the Axe Valley Pedallers. On Tuesdays, home-cooked, two-course lunches are served at 12.30 pm at the bargain price of £6 per person. We continue past the Old Granary, Old Forge

and Jubilee House (built by Mrs Evans of Forde Abbey as a village library and reading room). The water pump here has a tap for filling our water bottles. Turning right we admire a row of pretty terraced stone cottages. Opposite is Golden House, formerly the Golden Lion Inn.

Heading southwest out of Thorncombe towards Holditch, at Thorncombe Thorn roundel we go straight on, then bear right at Shearing Cross. Through the hamlet of School House, School House Farm is on our right, where the poorhouse was situated, and the Schoolhouse itself is on the left. Ignoring an unsigned left turn, we continue on past the red signpost, one of only four in Dorset, its single arm directing people towards the hamlet of Hewood.

After about half a mile we turn left towards Holditch. There's a simple bench seat here with amazing views northwest towards Chard. We bear right at the Old Forge, then on down past Manor Farm, and take the third left, signed Hawkchurch (the finger sign to Hawkchurch is missing but the other two fingers are present). Bearing left at Yardleigh Cross, then again at Castle Cross, we start the climb into Hawkchurch, past its stone cross.

The village is near the Somerset border and was formally transferred from Dorset to Devon in 1896. It has a well-stocked community shop behind the village hall serving drinks and snacks. The tower of St John the Baptist Church seems imposing as it's quite near the road, and

the churchyard is particularly attractive, if noticeably lacking in gravestones. Opposite is the Old Inn; a coaching house and hostelry has been on the site since 1543.

We meet the B3165 and between signs for Devon on our right and Dorset on our left we go straight on through decorative white gates towards Wootton Fitzpaine. A runner stops to help us with directions and recommends the food at the Bottle Inn at Marshwood, about a mile away to the left. Booze and bikes don't mix, but this pub sounds interesting, especially as it's the venue for the annual World Nettle Eating Championships. In this hour-long event, the winner is the contestant who eats the leaves from the greatest number of 2-ft-long stalks. Rolling the nettles first or dipping them in beer is said to help reduce the eye-watering pain. Nettles are rich in iron and vitamin C and have been used for centuries in making soup, teas and beers. But eating them raw has disagreeable consequences. Tongues turn black and subsequent bowel movements are not for the faint hearted.

We head down through Charmouth Forest (which seems to be a collective name for a number of different plantations). This is a pleasant road with beech woods either side and plenty of parking places for enjoying a walk. This area and Wyld Warren are popular with foragers and groups from River Cottage.

Down the hill we ignore the road to Fishpond and bear right to Wootton Fitzpaine following NCN Route 2. Reaching a T-junction, we turn right towards Charmouth. At the village hall, a sign reads 'This clock and bell were erected in memory of those from this parish who fell in the Great War. Their names are in the church'. The church is rather a trek though, about a mile away in the grounds of the manor house.

We take the left fork towards Charmouth through Catherston Leweston. The short slog uphill rewards us with sea views. At the stone entrance to Catherston Manor we walk up the drive to St Mary's Church, formerly the chapel for the Manor. ***There is no parking or turning at the church but ample space to park off-road near the entrance.*** St Mary's is one of only three churches in Dorset still with its original oak pews and ceiling.

On down the hill, the lane crosses a bridge over the A35 before entering Charmouth, where we go right and then left to follow the sign to the beach. We find a bench sheltered from the wind where we enjoy lunch surrounded by some of the best coastal views in Dorset, with Lyme Regis off to our right and Golden Cap left. The Heritage Centre, once a cement factory, has fascinating displays and popular fossil walks, and anyone wanting to go on one of the walks would be wise to book ahead.

Reluctantly, we bid farewell to Charmouth's considerable charms and pedal back past the tennis club, the oldest in Dorset. Founded in the early 1880s as a croquet club with two lawns, tennis initially took second place. Until well after WWII, only high-ranking service officers, landed gentry, doctors, lawyers and those of independent means were permitted to join. Four Whittington sisters – direct descendants of Dick Whittington, Lord Mayor of London – appear to have reigned as 'Queen Bees' in Charmouth for almost 70 years. Beryl, Winnie, Dorothy and Joan (all spinsters) controlled the tennis club for the first half of the 20th century, dictating to other members whom they might play. The club closed on Sundays, and on all other days play stopped at 4 o'clock prompt for tea!

We head east out of Charmouth, past the big caravan parks, up to the A35, where we go right, but only for 150 m, then left towards Whitchurch Canonicorum. We pass the village hall, formerly the 'National School' dated 1840. On the last Sunday in January the hall hosts Farmhouse Breakfast Week, an annual campaign aimed at encouraging people to make time for a hearty breakfast. No bacon sarnies on offer today though, so instead we help ourselves to a few russet apples which some kind person has left in a box at a garden gate. One of the joys of cycling is that we are travelling slowly enough to notice home-grown produce.

The church of St Candida and Holy Cross in Whitchurch Canonicorum is the only church in England, apart from Westminster Abbey, to contain an original shrine with relics of a saint. Saint Wite is thought to have lived during the 9th century as a hermit or holy woman on the cliff-top above the village. She is said to have maintained fires to act as beacons for sailors. After her death she was buried in the church. It was thought her relics had healing powers and many pilgrims travelled hundreds of miles to this quiet place. More recently, the murdered Bulgarian dissident Georgi Markov was buried in the churchyard and his headstone reads 'Died In the Cause of Freedom'. He was stabbed with a poisoned umbrella on Waterloo

Bridge in 1978 and his killer was never brought to justice. Markov's mother-in-law lived nearby and his wife's family goes back several generations in West Dorset. The ashes of veteran broadcaster Sir Robin Day are interred close to the church door, commemorated with a headstone inscribed 'In Loving Memory of Sir Robin Day – the Grand Inquisitor', who died in 2000. Margaret Thatcher greeted the news of his death by saying, 'Our paths often crossed and I always enjoyed the joust'. Sir Robin had a home nearby.

After the church we bear left towards Ryall, then left again at the Five Bells Inn. We begin a bit of a climb towards Shave Cross with its 14th-century thatched inn. The village name dates back to the Middle Ages, when Catholic pilgrim monks and priests would stop here to have their hair shaved as a mark of respect before going on to visit St Wite's shrine (the old inn sign used to depict this procedure, known as tonsure). We're pretty much central to the Marshwood Vale here.

At the inn we turn left, and then at Allviews Cottage go right towards Pilsdon. A detour takes us to St Mary's Church in the grounds of Pilsdon Community. Founded in 1958, this private community, situated in a Jacobean manor house, provides refuge for people in crisis, such as bereavement, drug dependence or alcoholism, or of fragile mental health. Wayfarers and the homeless are offered accommodation on a temporary basis. A common life of prayer, meals and work (in the gardens, farm or house) provides a structure in which people can begin to rebuild their lives. The day begins at 7.25 a.m. and lights

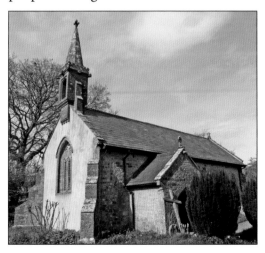

out is at 9.45 p.m. No alcohol is allowed. A description of the community soon after its foundation still holds true: 'It attempts to offer unconditional friendship to all who come, however defeated and broken and near the end of their tether they may be.' The community holds services in the small adjoining church three times a day. Participation is encouraged but not obligatory. The church is simple, with plain flagstones, a piano and three wooden candelabra. No pews, just a few chairs with cushions but mostly straw bales. There is a remarkable atmosphere of serenity.

From Pilsdon we follow signs for Broadwindsor, and after a gritty little climb meet the B3164. There's a layby to our left with an information board, and the 180-degree view over the Marshwood Vale is quite spectacular. The low, bowl-shaped area is surrounded by four hills over 200 m, including Dorset's two highest, Lewesdon Hill and Pilsdon Pen directly behind us. At 279 m, Lewesdon is the higher by just 2 m! We turn right on the B3164 for a short way, then left along unmarked Specket Lane. This brings us onto the B3165 at Blackdown. The Jubilee Trail and Monarch's Way both pass here, the latter a 615-mile walk which closely follows the route taken by 21-year-old King Charles II in 1651 as he fled, having lost the Battle of Worcester to Cromwell's New Model Army. We turn right, then immediately left at Cole's Cross, signed Winsham and Chard. Blackdown Hill is on our right. At Venn Chapel we take a peek at the wonderfully natural small graveyard (the chapel itself is now a private residence so discretion is required).

We head left towards Thorncombe and whizz down through Synderford and over the small river. Artist and printmaker Harry Banks lived here at Synderford House for more than 40 years during the interwar period, probably due to his friendship with the great artist Lucien Pissarro who also loved the West Country and lived at nearby Hewood. Banks used to work in a studio in the grounds of his home, surrounded by the lovely greenery and little streams. He designed Edward VII's coronation invitation card, and also owned the first wireless set in the village.

Climbing up into Thorncombe, we pass a house on the left called the Old Bakery next door to Halfpenny Bun Cottage. We are soon confronted by

a steep main street which reminds us of Devon – perhaps unsurprisingly, as this village was in that county until 1844 and borders both Devon and Somerset. By the cross we enter the churchyard and push the tandem along the path towards a bench. The dedication reads 'June's Singing Seat. Fond

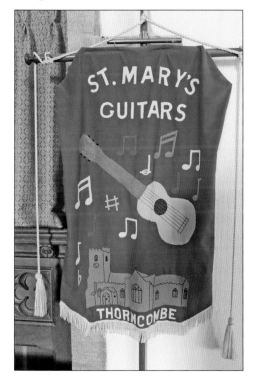

Memories of June "The Tune" Ede 1928–2009. She loved this village, this church, and the people in it. Come and quiet be and let the silence sing'.

After a brief rest, we go into the church, where we chat to some ladies arranging flowers for the Harvest Festival service. Allan notices a disc on the wall for 'St Mary's Guitars'. In 1977 this group of musicians recorded an album of Christian songs performed in the church. June Ede was a member and wrote many of the songs in their repertoire. Several were performed at her funeral. The group is still going strong and plays regularly at services and festivals in St Mary's and neighbouring churches.

# Route 2 – Beaminster

*(visiting Netherbury, Pymore, Bridport, Symondsbury,
Stoke Abbott, Broadwindsor and Chedington)*

**Distance:** 26 miles (42 km)

**Hills:** 530 m elevation change, three significant hills

**OS map:** Explorer 116 and 117

**Brief description:** Sunken lanes lead to villages steeped in history, with a couple
of museums on this route. Rivers and mills are reminiscent of earlier industries
revolving around local wool and flax. We follow in the footsteps of
school children and within sound of a curfew bell. We are spoilt
for choice with pubs and local stores.

In 1284 Beaminster was granted a charter for a market once a week and a
three-day fair in September; although there is no regular market here today.
The Square is a popular meeting place, with its 1906 covered market cross/
memorial, known locally as 'Julia', erected by Vincent Robinson of Parnham
House in memory of his sister.

From here we head southeast on the A3066 towards Melplash and Bridport, with the River Brit running along below the right side of the road. There are a couple of properties with coaching arches hinting at former use. After about 600 m we turn right, signed Netherbury.

Since leaving Beaminster we have had Parnham Park to our right. The house is well hidden from the road, but there are glimpses of the pretty deer park. It was the home of William Barnard Rhodes-Moorhouse, the first airman to receive the Victoria Cross. It was bought by furniture designer and maker John Makepeace in 1976, who founded Parnham Trust and the School for Craftsmen in Wood here. The Trust moved to nearby Hooke Park in 2000 (see Route 3) and the house was sold to Austrian financier Michael Treichl in 2001. After a £10 million restoration, the Elizabethan Grade I Listed Parnham House was ravaged by fire in 2017. Following Treichl's death, after suffering severe depression, Parnham is awaiting another wealthy buyer with the funds to restore it again. Towards the bottom of Crook Hill a mill stone marks the entrance to the old mill. The valley used to contain several mills to process flax used in the rope-making industry at Bridport.

We cycle on down the lane and cross the River Brit into Netherbury (signed Waytown). The 17th-century bridge has three dissimilar arches, the large round eastern one built for the mill race. We pass the former Star Inn, now a private house, but with its old sign over the door. When Victoria came to the throne the village had a population of around 2000 and there were at least six pubs, but now there is just the Hare & Hounds in nearby Waytown.

On up the hill past two former school buildings, we go right at the cottage with tall arched windows and pay a visit to the church, which stands on a hillside looking down over the village. St Mary's is a 'Small Pilgrim Place', one of only two in Dorset, the other being St Peter's in Langton Herring. Such churches highlight the importance of quiet prayer, encouragement, thoughtful conversation, rest and relaxation.

Back down Tower Hill, we turn right towards Waytown. We pass a drive leading to 17th-century Slape Manor Estate, probably best known for its former game-keeper's lodge named River Cottage, rented by Hugh Fearnley-Whittingstall, when he rose to fame as a celebrity chef in the 1990s. The main house has a library believed to have been designed by the young Thomas Hardy, who originally trained as an architect before becoming the famous writer.

We continue down Slape Hill, with a deep section of sunken lane, and on through Waytown. The Hare & Hounds has great views across the valley from its pub garden. We pass a right turn to Salwayash and proceed on through the hamlet of Wooth – apparently the River Brit was originally called the River Wooth. At Ebenezer Corner T-junction with Pymore Lane we turn left towards Bridport on NCN Route 2. We go over Watford Bridge, then right towards Pymore, passing the Pymore Inn. Just after the pub we detour right down Thread Mill Lane, past the old rope-working buildings. We're looking for the millpond, which I'd read was once a favourite place for punting and fishing and during the coldest winters even transformed into a skating rink, attracting crowds from miles around, once a 'vibrant scene of winter revelry'. Pymore dates back to the 14th century, when it had a flour mill powered by the river. By the 1700s the village was well established as a centre for rope making and it continued to grow and thrive over the next couple of centuries. Almost everyone in the village worked at the rope factory, and in the early 1900s Pymore had its own school, brewery and employee housing. A hostel built

for working girls was still going strong in the 1930s. The advent of man-made fibres forced the rope works to close in 1955. Most employees moved away in search of work, leaving Pymore derelict. The site was sold for development in the 1980s, although building didn't start until the 21st century. The new estate comprises cottages

rebuilt from original stone and apartments converted from dilapidated warehouses. The hostel has been transformed into three substantial houses.

A downside of the rope industry was pollution of the River Brit, which has also suffered more recently from invasive Himalayan balsam. However, water conditions are improving, and fish passes have encouraged salmon and trout, supporting wildlife such as kingfishers and otters. I stay with the tandem while Allan goes in search of the millpond, but he returns with the disappointing news that although the pond is still there, it has been largely swallowed up by reeds.

Back on Pymore Road (which becomes Victoria Grove) we enter Bridport. The very last 100-m section of Victoria Grove is no-entry, so we wiggle left along Chards Mead Road, then right along North Street. There we turn right onto West Street, and on our left is the Ropemakers pub. The town was built around the rope and net industry, dating back to the 9th century, the local area being perfect for growing flax and hemp. The rope was used for hangmen's nooses (and subsequently nicknamed a 'Bridport dagger') and during Henry VIII's time it was ordered that 'all cordage for the English Navy should, for a limited time, be made at Bridport or within 5 miles of it and nowhere else'. Joseph Gundry established a business in 1665, and the family name is still closely linked to the town. Bridport produced the goal nets for England's 1966 World Cup and has been the official supplier to Wimbledon since the 1870s. The town's museum is based in a 16th-century building donated by Captain Codd to the borough council in 1932. It houses a rope and net collection with working machinery, Roman jewellery, amulets and armour, and fossils from the nearby Jurassic Coast, and explains a dark period of disease, decay and death. There is a popular street market on Wednesday and Saturday, and Palmers Brewery at the bottom of town is worth a visit. Established in 1794, it apparently has Britain's only thatched brewery building, and there is an impressive old waterwheel.

We head west on the B3162 out of Bridport and at the mini roundabout notice a sign for butcher RJ Balson & Son. This is the oldest continually trading 'family' business in the UK, trading since 1515 and currently on its 26th generation. After crossing the River Simene, we turn right signed Symondsbury on Duck Street. We soon pass Symondsbury Estate Bike Park. The ever-expanding Estate seems to have something for all, with an eatery and retail outlets including the very helpful Bridport Cycles. The main landmark here though is conical, tree-topped Colmer's Hill. It's only 417 ft high, so seemingly without much to brag about, but this well-loved little hill has been climbed, painted, photographed and written about umpteen times over the years. The ascent is steady but quite steep and at the top there is a trig point

and coastal views of West Dorset and East Devon. The school building has an air of Victorian authority. Founded in 1868 on the site of the village poor house, its first headmaster was a man named William Kennett who had recently returned from 2 years in Australia working as a missionary.

We go northeast out of the village along Mill Lane. Just before the left corner is an old sheep wash. We head towards Moorbath and Broadoak, climbing adjacent to Old Warren Hill, along a road cut deeply into the hillside with limestone on either side and vegetation growing up and over to form a rather atmospheric 'tunnel'. Over the top we are rewarded by a scenic descent.

On to Broadoak and at the T-junction we stop to look in the phone box, which has a sign saying 'Welcome to Cyclists and Walkers. Do call in for information and stuff'. Inside are a pump and puncture repair outfit and local leaflets and guides. We turn left signed Shave Cross and Marshwood on NCN Route 2. We stop at New House Pottery, simply because it looks intriguing, surrounded by chickens and ducks. It turns out to be a small co-operative of four potters who make a range of items. We find a couple of mugs we like and fortunately have enough money to buy them. When cycling we often only take a few pounds with us. I'm the frugal one in our relationship and nothing pleases me more than to arrive home after a great day on the tandem without having spent so much as a penny, although I do find it hard to let an ice-cream opportunity pass me by.

Continuing on, we take the right turn towards Stoke Abbott, where two locals are renovating the finger post. We pass through Lower Monkwood to a T-junction with Blackney Cottage ahead, where we turn right. Someone has done a wonderful job of carving an old tree trunk into a huge owl.

The road climbs steeply here, treating us to views of Pilsdon Pen and Marshwood Vale to the left and Lewesdon Hill straight ahead. We cross the B3162 at Four Ashes junction, with a more close-up view of Dorset's highest point to our left. We drop down past Brimley Farm, then uphill again into Stoke Abbott. Here we take a break in St Mary's churchyard, sitting on a bench close to an impressive yew tree. A tombstone just outside the south door was used as a dole table in the 18th century. Wealthy people often left provision in their wills for money or food to be distributed from dole tables annually to the poor, generally on a Saint's Day or perhaps at Easter. This is probably the origin of the phrase 'on the dole'. I'm amused to see a sign beside the door reading 'Please close porch gates when sheep are in the churchyard'. There were no sheep that day but we could see and hear them in an adjoining field. Inside the church I spot a small brass wall tablet commemorating Evelyn Jane Wakely who played the organ here every Sunday (with only the very occasional absence) from 1907 to 1963 and was also the sub-postmistress for 38 years. There's a pretty painted plaque 'Dedicated to the memory of Caroline Lucy Andrews died 30th May 1920. For 22 years the most excellent Matron of Beaminster Union House, by the Guardians, their co-workers

and others in the district'. On 25August 1899, *Bridport News* reported that Mrs Andrews was among members of staff who took children on an outing to West Bay. Yet only 50 years previously, inmates of the workhouse were severely treated. On 21 March 1843, the Pauper Offence Book records Mary Bartlett being sent to prison for 2 months after breaking a window. Offences against property received harsh punishment in the mid-19th century.

Stoke Abbott is one of the few villages where a curfew bell is still rung. In medieval times this tolled in villages throughout the land as darkness fell to remind people to extinguish their lights and fires. Most houses were built of wood and could catch fire easily. In Stoke Abbott there was a long tradition of ringing the bell at 7 am and 7 pm specifically for farm workers. But times change and now the bell rings from May to September at 8 am, Monday to Friday.

Setting off again, we turn right out of the church and at the next junction notice a well with a stone lion head spouting water from the hillside. We turn left here at an old workshop, signed Broadwindsor. It's

rather steep so we're soon off the tandem, pushing up the shadowy lane cut through the limestone, with ferns and bracken either side and a canopy of trees overhead

At the top we meet the B3162 again and go right into Broadwindsor. In essence it's the meeting place of five roads, with a one-way system at its centre which keeps things moving. It's a well-visited place because of the popular and multifaceted Broadwindsor Craft Centre, with its range of sellers and popular eatery. Just after the White Lion Inn, we pause at King Charles Cottage, as, like several other West Dorset villages, Broadwindsor sheltered the king as he fled from Cromwell's Army. Disguised as a servant, the king took refuge at the Castle Inn, which later burnt down in 1856.

Broadwindsor Community Stores opened in 2013, described as 'a triumph of local endeavor and a major achievement for Broadwindsor and the surrounding villages'. It was requested by over 90% of residents in the Parish Plan, so is well supported by locals, though it took a lot of effort to realise. It's located in the old Telephone Exchange on Drimpton Road, next to the school. Seventeenth-century worshippers at the church of St John the Baptist seem to have been fortunate. Their vicar, known as 'quaint old Tom Fuller', was a jovial parson who preached witty sermons to a congregation overflowing with chuckling parishioners. Nowadays the clergy are permitted to indulge in a little cautious humour, but in 17th-century Britain, levity of any sort was generally unheard of.

At Cross Keys roundel junction we bear left and follow the one-way system to the turning to Mosterton. After a few hundred metres up the steep lane we turn left again opposite a modern timber-built house. At Littlewindsor we turn right, then drop down the hill and turn left towards Mosterton. At the A3066, we go left through Mosterton. Next to the village hall, the Old Gospel Hall looks rather cute. We cross the River Axe and pass the village shop. The church is hidden away on the left, and opposite is the

Admiral Hood pub, formerly the New Inn and renamed after the distinguished naval family who lived in the village from the 16th century. After the pub we turn right up the initially narrow Chedington Lane. This road is hilly in places but affords great views on both sides. After a few miles we take the steep left fork opposite Broadleaze Farm and drop down into Lower Chedington. Lower Farm has an impressively long thatched roof, and an outbuilding has a wonderful old AA sign.

The road snakes around former St James Church, and then beside a long wall, behind which is the gable end and bell tower of Chedington Court. Ahead we pass a post marking the start of the 47-mile-long River Parrett Trail. At the north end of the village is Winyards Gap cutting, with its similarly named inn. The woods here were donated to the National Trust in 1949 in memory of the 43rd (Wessex) Division soldiers who died in WWII. A stone pillar was erected in 1952, a replica of the one near Hill 112 near Caen in

Normandy, the site of the Division's first major battle in 1944. It has views over Dorset, Devon, Somerset and Wiltshire, the four counties that made up the Division.

We turn right onto the A356 signed Maiden Newton, and climb up through the 'Gap'. This can be quite a busy road, so cyclists should take care. However, it's only about a mile until Corscombe Cross junction, where we turn right signed Beaminster. After some undulations, we go straight over the crossroads and drop down the 1-in-5 hill from Beaminster Down into town.

Beaminster Museum is accommodated in a former Methodist chapel, and one of its permanent exhibitions is dedicated to the history of education in Beaminster. When she died in 1682, wealthy spinster Frances Tucker left money to pay for a schoolmaster to teach 20 poor boys, with instructions that he should be dismissed if he proved to be negligent, loud or debauched. Beaminster Grammar School, known later as Beaminster and Netherbury Grammar School, took boarders and day boys and eventually opened its

doors to girls too. Day pupils were served their midday meal in the nearby Red Lion Inn. There are reports of midnight pranks in the 1950s, with pupils sneaking off for moonlit walks and cycle rides. An exceptionally daring boy took a girl to West Bay on the crossbar of his bicycle, risking a severe caning from the headmaster. A blue plaque on the right gable end of School Cottage facing School House Close commemorates the grammar school that operated here from 1868 to 1962.

At the museum you can also find out about the history of linen and woollen manufacture, using locally grown flax and wool. The tower of St Mary's Church, one of the highest in Dorset at 100 ft, has carvings of a mill and a man with a fuller's bat – 'fulling' being the pummeling of wet cloth to remove the natural wool grease or lanolin and any remaining dirt.

In the 18th century Beaminster was the boyhood home of arctic explorer, naturalist and author Samuel Hearne, believed to be an inspiration for Samuel Taylor Coleridge's *The Rime of the Ancient Mariner*. Today's most famous resident is actor Martin Clunes, who hosts Buckham Fair, a vintage-themed dog and pony show, near his family's farm. Since it started in 2009, the event has raised over £623,000 for local charities. Martin can often be seen riding his Clydesdale horses around Beaminster. The annual Beaminster Festival of music, theatre, art and literature has also been popular since it started in 1996.

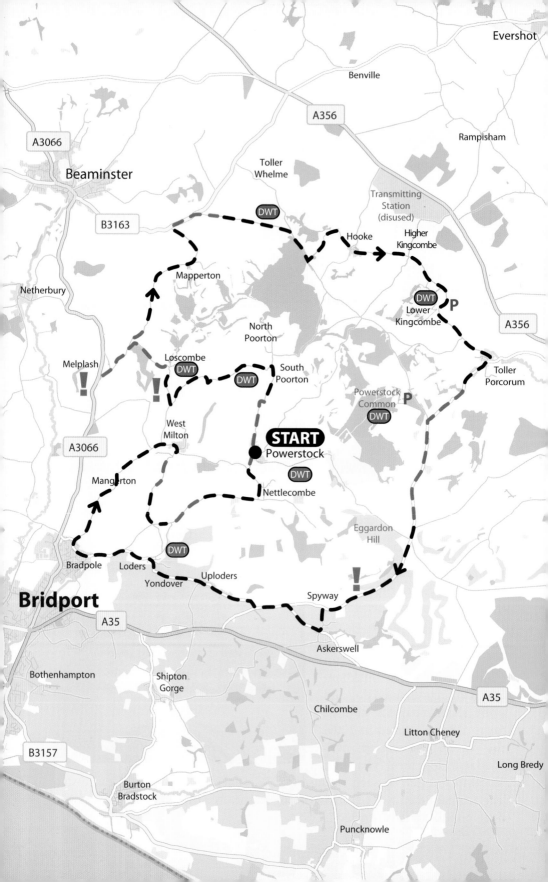

# Route 3 –Powerstock

*(visiting Mapperton, Kingcombe, Eggardon,*
*Loders, Mangerton and West Milton)*

**Distance:** 24 miles (39 km)

**Hills:** 600 m elevation change, two significant hills

**OS map:** Explorer 116 and 117

**Brief description:** We pass an old mill, following winding rivers and DWT nature reserves. In the 'Nation's Finest Manor House' we discover the origins of the bacon butty and stroll around a garden full of variety. On Dead Man's Lane we find a sycamore sapling planted in memory of a deadly 16th-century dispute between neighbours. A no-through road leads to a remote and lovely hamlet.

From the church and school in Powerstock we head north towards Poorton, up rather testing Dugberry Hill. Poorton is a tiny hamlet with two churches – one in ruins and another with an unusual open spire. From South Poorton we almost double back onto Ridgeback Lane, heading towards West Milton. We soon pass DWT South Poorton Nature Reserve, with its steep wildflower-rich grassland and wet woodland within a hidden valley.

At the staggered crossroads which is Lancombes Cross we turn right to Loscombe, a tiny hamlet with several farms. Cyclists should take care on this narrow steep lane, especially after heavy rain. We cross a ford, which is dry today, but there's a functional wooden bridge should it be needed. The main feature here is another DWT reserve, that of Loscombe. Its 3.7-mile-long Ant Hill Trail is named after the mounds that have developed over many years which are the nests of yellow meadow ants, and indicate undisturbed grassland.

Climbing out of Loscombe, we meet a T-junction, where our route leads us right, but it's just a short distance downhill to Melplash so we detour to investigate. The Half Moon Inn has a plaque commemorating the 150th anniversary of Melplash Agricultural Society. In 1846 two farmers held a ploughing match to determine whose ploughman was the best. Each bet £5, a substantial sum at that time, and after the event local farmers and landowners feasted in the Half Moon (then the Melplash Inn) and agreed to

form Melplash Agricultural Society and to hold an annual ploughing contest. This is one of the largest agricultural shows in the southwest, now held on showgrounds between Bridport and West Bay. Attached to the pub is the Old School House, and next door is the 19th-century church. When opened, a notice stated that all church seating should be free. For centuries before that it was the custom to rent pews and people began to think they had a right to sit in a particular place. Some even screwed ownership plates to 'their' pew. The rent was important to church income, and the position and quality of individual pews were crucial to the social standing of wealthy families. This resulted in the poor being forced to perch uncomfortably on benches and stools. Today a glass screen divides the church in two. The pews have been removed from one side to form a social meeting place, which is also laid out for a badminton court. The other side is used for regular worship.

We retrace our steps from Melplash, back past the Loscombe turning. After about 1 km, we pause at a young sycamore tree at the corner of what is known as Dead Man's Lane. This tree is the replacement for the old Posy Tree which died and was taken down in 2011 (see page 29). On a little further we visit Mapperton House. It is beautifully positioned and surrounded by hills and ancient pastureland. We cycle down a long gravel track leading to a car park and the elegant Ham-stone manor house with mullioned windows, balustrades and twisted chimneys. Mapperton is first mentioned in the *Domesday Book* of 1086. Over 900 years later in 2006, it was chosen as 'The Nation's Finest Manor House' in a *Country Life* competition. It's lunchtime so we make our way to the café, which can be accessed separately from the house and gardens. Since we are visiting the family home of the Earl and Countess of Sandwich (the Earl allegedly being the first person to slap a slice of meat between two hunks of bread and make a meal of it), we decide it's only right to order a couple of sarnies.

We head off for a tour of the house and history of the family. This isn't something we often do, partly because we're never dressed like normal people. As soon as we're off the tandem I feel a little self-conscious in cycling shorts. The house featured in the 2015 film *Far From the Madding Crowd*, 1996 adaptation of Jane Austen's *Emma* and the TV version of *Tom Jones*, with Brian Blessed playing the part of Squire Western. Afterwards we explore the gardens, where there is a 17th-century croquet lawn and pavilion. Stone steps lead to an Italian Arts and Crafts garden, with grottoes, ornamental birds, fountains and orangery. This is a peaceful place, with a surprise around almost every corner and great views. We stroll through a formal paved area with topiary yew and box, then a lower terrace with ponds. Beyond is a jungly area, with a grassy trail beside a stream. Magnolias, camellias and rhododendrons bloom here.

A medieval church lies alongside the house. It's usually locked but a key is available from the ticket office. All Saints was made redundant in 1977 and became part of the manor house, but occasional services are held in summer and on major festivals. In the churchyard is a seat 'In Memory of Bernard Ralph Cox, organist of this parish 1908–1978', a remarkable achievement. Among the few graves can be found one for a former owner of Mapperton, Mrs Ethel Labouchere.

The reason so few people are buried here is that All Saints is sited on shallow, rock-hard ground, making burials almost impossible. So there was an agreement that Mapperton's dead could be buried in Netherbury churchyard for an annual fee of 3d. Funeral parties carried the deceased up the aptly named Dead Man's Lane and a few miles across the hill to Netherbury for burial. This worked well until the Black Death in 1582, which devastated much of rural Dorset. Residents of Netherbury, fearing infection, forced Mapperton mourners to turn back and dig a pit as a communal grave on the slopes of nearby Warren Hill. Human bones still sometimes surface here. Just about everyone in Mapperton ended up in the mass grave and the village itself never recovered, leaving only the manor house and a few scattered farms and houses. The sycamore Posy Tree we saw earlier marks the spot where the dead were collected before their final journey to Warren Hill. Grieving families carried posies of herbs and flowers in an attempt to mask the reek of putrefaction and believing that this might protect them against disease. Mourners would drop their posies underneath the tree on their way back from the burial.

Leaving Mapperton House, we continue along the lane to reach the B3163. Turning right, we begin to climb Storridge Hill towards Maiden Newton, but after 400 m a sign to Hooke takes us right up a slight rise and then down past the left turn to Toller Whelme. *Toller* is the original name of the River Hooke and *Whelme* is Old English for source or spring. Allan professes himself in love with this pretty village and is all for selling up and moving here. We regularly play this game on holiday, especially when we are in some beautiful part of the country where property prices are temptingly affordable. The thatched manor house faces south towards surrounding hills, and has stone-mullioned windows looking out over a stream and lake, complete with stone-built boathouse. In the 17th century, the estate passed into the possession

of George Penne from East Coker near Yeovil, and for a while the village became known as Pinny's Toller or Penne Toller. A hundred years or so later it was taken over by the wealthy Pope family and, as a pious man, William Pope paid for a church to be built to fulfill a promise he made at the time of his mother's death in 1828 when she was too ill to manage the 3-mile journey to Corscombe church. The occasional service is still held here at St John's Church.

There's a small and rather wet DWT reserve at the southeast end of the hamlet. *Hooke* is a derivation of *hoc*, Old English for 'sharp bend in a stream', and the river does curve considerably here so this may explain its change of name. Dorset-born author and broadcaster Ralph Wightman (see Route 8) described the area as 'many springy and boggy patches which are not typical of chalk valleys' – the reason being that the stream has eroded down to the greensand below.

We continue down the lane, passing Hooke Park, its impressive entrance gate sculptures revealing it as the 142-acre Architectural Association's Woodland School site. The designated ancient woodland here was historically a deer hunting estate, and today is renowned for glorious swathes of bluebells in spring. We take the first left into Hooke, passing Hooke Court, a specialist educational residential centre which can also be hired for holidays and special events. A little further on, we pause beside a large well-kept pond watching the activity of dragonflies, damselflies, moorhens and ducks. Writing in 1965, Ralph Wightman commented that at Hooke village itself 'the largest spring I have ever seen used to gush out of the steep hillside, and was immediately used for watercress'. Maps show the watercress beds are now disused, and, although not obvious to the passer-by, they have been replaced by fish farming. Family business Hooke Springs supplies brown and rainbow trout for rivers and lakes throughout England. Careful feeding means 'not only do our fish taste wonderful, but they look beautiful and fight like tigers'.

Continuing on through the village, near the church we go straight on at the staggered crossroads towards Kingcombe. At Higher Kingcombe Lodge there are more spring-fed lakes, this time available for coarse fishing and stocked with carp (mirror, common and ghost), perch, roach, rudd, bream and tench. Down the lane we come to the Kingcombe Centre, show-piece of the DWT, which offers events and courses ranging from painting and willow weaving to residential weekends and walking tours. The countryside and farmland here are carefully conserved as they have been for centuries, and the centre has a tearoom open to the public.

At a T-junction we turn right and visit the church of Toller Porcorum dedicated to St Andrew and St Peter. In the tower hang two bells, one carved with the word PEACE and the other with THANKSGIVING FOR MERCY, commemorating the safe return of local men who fought in WWII. My dad lived in the village as a child and I'm curious to see if there are any family graves in the churchyard. Sadly not, but it's a peaceful place and we sit for a few minutes on a bench placed 'In Loving Memory of Frank Churchill Walbridge'. Walbridge families have farmed here for generations. The whole of

Kingcombe Farm (about 640 acres), which is now the Kingcombe Centre, came on the market in 1985 following the death of the owner Arthur Walbridge, aged 90.

We continue through the village, crossing an old metal-sided railway bridge. Closed in 1975, this was the 1857 Maiden Newton to Bridport branch line, off the main Castle Cary–Weymouth line. Recently the section from Powerstock Common to Loders and a short stretch outside

*View west at Eggardon Hill.*

Maiden Newton have become a cycle path. Unfortunately, other stretches have been subsumed into private properties and some landowners are unwilling to open up this potential leisure route. On a brighter note, local resident Vanora Hereward, a retired solicitor, village hall trustee and bell ringer, who died in 2012, generously donated land next to her home. She helped set up a community trust to develop it, securing planning permission for five affordable homes enabling local families to continue living in the village, and a new post office. She died before it was completed, but the development is named Hereward Close after her.

We climb steadily out of the village to the T-junction with Barrowland Lane. Just downhill to our right is the main entrance to DWT Powerstock Common, but today we turn left signed Askerswell. We pass the left turn for Wynford Eagle, and to our right enjoy our first view of Eggardon Hill. We go straight over the next crossroads towards Askerswell. There's a trig point near the road, then the main access path onto Eggardon Hill and its Iron Age hillfort, with fantastic views west across Lyme Bay. No wonder residents of Maiden Newton and Frome Vauchurch chose this place for a special village picnic on 22 June 1897 to celebrate Queen Victoria's Diamond Jubilee. Today the northern half is private, but the National Trust owns the southern part. Archaeological finds in the area date back to the Neolithic period. Seven Bronze Age axes were found southwest of Eggardon Hill, believed to be a merchant's hoard as they were unsharpened.

Just after the Askerswell village sign, and before the Spyway Inn, a smugglers' haunt *c* 1600, we turn left down School Lane. The pub garden has great views south across the valley, and CAMRA awarded it Best Pub Garden of the Year 2017. We pass the Old School which closed in 1965 and is now a private house. It opened in 1857 as a local initiative, became an elementary

school in 1871 and was enlarged in 1901 but often suffered from truancy. Recollections of school and village life are recorded in the Askerswell Millennium Folder. The village won Best Kept Small Village in 1993, 1999, 2002, 2005 and 2016 – the badges and a bench are proudly displayed at the junction near Askers House.

We turn right at the crossroads, and on our right is the fledgling River Asker, which the Environment Agency has classed as 'poor' because of a lack of fish and aquatic plants. There is no single body responsible for improving the quality of the watercourse, so the Dorset AONB, DWT and Farming and Wildlife Advisory Group have come together to help communities along the river identify problems that need fixing and plan works to overcome them. The main problems identified are artificial barriers, riparian trees, catchment land use, agricultural nutrients and invasive species. A similar 'community' approach is being used to prevent flooding in Winterbourne Abbas (see Route 5).

We carry on back to rejoin the Spyway road, turning left signed Loders. We bear right, ignoring the left turn to Bridport, and enter Uploders. Directly ahead is a rather rustic sign for Collins Nets – a relatively modern business at only 30 years, but, as mentioned in Route 2, it's certainly a nod to the past, as Bridport and surrounding villages have been heavily involved with rope and net making since *c* 1200. Collins is based in an old dairy and the business produces netting for game rearing, fisheries industries, fish farms and Environment Agencies across the UK, and for golf courses. Further on, Uploders House has a lovely wrap-around canopy veranda, and until 2012 the next building round the S-bend had a local rope and net museum, which has since transferred to Bridport Museum. They are prevalent in West Dorset, but there's a particularly fine display of strip lynchets on the hillside just south of the Crown Inn. Sandwiched between the two 'Loders' is Yondover, where the road crosses the River Asker.

We enter Loders under the disused railway bridge, and the village school is on our left. This opened in 1869 on land owned by the Nepean family of Loders Court, and was originally called Lady Nepean's School. Not to be outdone by Askerswell, Loders won Best Small Village in 2014, with plaques

on the school frontage. The front is traditional Victorian, with porch and bell tower, but the rear has a very modern look. There is a well in the playground, with a smugglers' tunnel entrance within the well.

We continue past the Loders Arms, now the sole pub, but two doors down is the former Farmers Arms, which closed in 1973 and is now a private house. At the church gate there is a sign advertising 'A Pint and a Ponder'. This regular informal discussion group rotates around the local pubs, with topics such as 'What is Community – and is technology killing it?' and 'Plastic – how do we reduce our consumption?' This and much more, covering a range of villages, is included on the excellent 'Eggardon and Colmers View' website. It's obviously an active and engaged community, with a busy WI and popular annual scarecrow competition.

We continue past the church, heading west. The last obvious building as we leave the village is Loders Court, built in 1799 for Sir Evan Nepean, a colonial administrator and ancestor of the actor Hugh Grant. Apparently part of the south wall is 13 ft thick, and there are signs of a tunnel leading towards the church, smuggling being rife hereabouts. The house is on the site of a 12th-century Benedictine priory founded by Baldwin de Redvers, 1st Earl of Devon, in the reign of King Henry I. It is thought monks from the abbey of St Marie de Montebourg in Normandy introduced cider-making to Dorset.

Cycling through Bradpole we ignore all left turnings until the junction with Townsend Way, where we turn right and soon reach Mangerton. We pass the entrance to Mangerton Mill, which has a working 17th-century water mill powered by a 12-ft overshot water wheel made of cast iron and oak. It was a grist and flax mill that last worked commercially in 1966. It also

packs in a Museum of Rural Bygones, tearoom, craft centre, art school and gallery, lakeside walk and small campsite.

At West Milton we pause at the busy little traffic island with its Millennium bus shelter. There were at least two pubs, the Red Lion and Leopard, but both are now private houses. The tower is all that remains of a medieval chapel dedicated to St Mary Magdalene that once stood here; it was dismantled and the rest of the stone taken to Powerstock and used to extend the parish school. Renowned writer and broadcaster Kenneth Allsop lived at Milton Mill and wrote *In the Country*, a collection of essays mostly about West Dorset. He died in 1973 and is buried in Powerstock churchyard.

We continue over Mangerton River and turn right signed Loders. The lane soon becomes 'sunken', dark and foreboding, and is quite a climb. At the staggered crossroads we turn left towards Nettlecombe, ignoring two right turns back to Loders, and climb up and over Welcome Hill. There are views ahead to Eggardon Hill again.

At the next crossroads, ahead is signed to 'Marsh Farm Only North Eggardon'. North Eggardon Farm once belonged to Isaac Gulliver, an infamous Dorset 18th-century smuggler. He planted a circle of trees on Eggardon Hill to act as a landmark for smuggling boats waiting to land contraband at West Bay, Burton Bradstock, Swyre and West Bexington. The luxury goods were often transported to fashionable Bath and Bristol. When revenue men cut down the trees, Gulliver moved his activities inland to Kinson, 5 miles from Bournemouth.

We turn left to Nettlecombe, passing the Marquis of Lorne pub. Then, at the sunken T-junction, we go right and wiggle up into Powerstock. There is the small DWT King's Lane Orchard Nature Reserve just up the lane towards Whetley, with remnants of the cider-apple orchards that used to be so important in this area. The last Powerstock Cider Festival was held in 2017, and over 16 years the mix of around 30 amateur and professional cider makers donating their time and cider has raised over £43,000 for local charities. The popular event has since transferred to Melplash. Just off Whetley Lane, Castle Hill is the site of a former motte and bailey hillfort. It was probably a hunting lodge used by King John who hunted on nearby Powerstock Common – now a DWT reserve of approximately 300 acres.

We are now back in Powerstock, a village we last visited some 30 years ago, when we stayed at the Three Horse Shoes – a lovely pub, though we passed a restless night because the nearby church clock chimed hourly. I know this can be a contentious issue in villages, with long-established residents exasperated by complaints from newcomers who can't sleep at night. I'd better keep out of that one! In the 19th century, Powerstock had a reputation as rather a rough place, and certainly the burials page in the Parish Register makes for intriguing reading: for example, Benjamin Legg died aged 64 on 11 September 1862: 'Probably worn out by drinking and hard living'. There was scandal too and accusations of murder. In 1839, following the suspicious deaths of a man and woman, an inquest was held in the Three Horse Shoes. Both bodies were exhumed and placed in the church, where a post-mortem was performed on the altar. St Mary's was closed for 3 weeks until it was fit for use again. Enough arsenic was found in the woman's body to have killed half a dozen people. Her husband was charged with murder but acquitted. The village hall is known as 'The Hut' as it was purchased just after WWI and used as Army accommodation. It was dismantled and re-erected on the current site next to the primary school, and has been well maintained, updated and used over its 100 years and more.

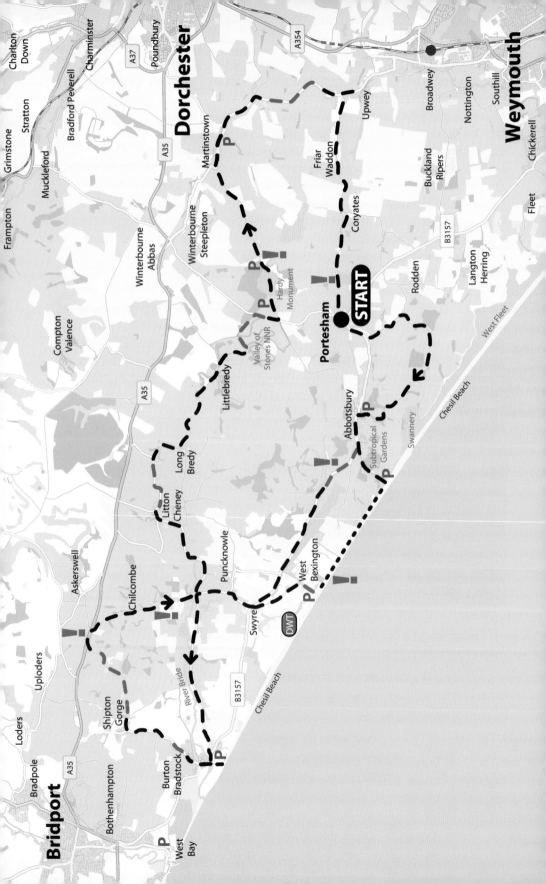

# Route 4 – Portesham

(visiting Abbotsbury, West Bexington, Puncknowle,
Long Bredy, Littlebredy and Martinstown)

**Distance:** 36 miles (58 km)

**Hills:** 830 m elevation change, three/four significant hills

**OS map:** Explorer 117 and OL15

**Brief description:** We enjoy dramatic coastal views, the *'Broadchurch'* waterfall and an inspiring cricket pitch. A valley of stones and the windswept Hardy Monument lead on down to an old wishing well and cat racing.

We begin our tour in Portesham, taking the B3157 west towards Abbotsbury. This is part of the scenic Jurassic Coast Road Drive and can be busy, so we take the first left signed West Elworth, a relatively untravelled lane affording great views across the Fleet. At about 8 miles long, the Fleet is the largest lagoon in England and is a wetland of international importance (Ramsar site) and SSSI.

We reach a T-junction and turn right. This is a narrow stretch of road and Allan pulls in close to the verge to let a car go past. Motorists appreciate courteous behaviour from cyclists and, to be fair, we don't want cars stuck behind us any more than they want to be there. After a while we reach Abbotsbury Swannery, the world's only managed colony of nesting mute swans (approximately 600). It was founded by monks in *c* 1393 and is now part of Ilchester Estates. There's mass feeding at noon and 4 pm daily, or you can time your visit to see the cygnets (usually mid-May to end of June). The Swannery also displays an early prototype 'Highball' bouncing bomb (of Dambusters fame), as the Fleet was used as a testing area during its development. Continuing up the lane we pass Abbotsbury Children's Farm, partly housed within a large thatched tithe barn, built by the monks in the 1390s.

Looking down on us are the Abbey ruins. Up the hill we meet the B3157 again, but it's slower here as the tight 90-degree corner between the buildings often holds up the traffic. On into the village, we pass Bride Valley Farm Shop which sells home-reared beef from their Dorset Longhorns grazed locally on land managed without chemicals. Abbotsbury is steeped in history and deservedly popular with tourists but delightfully quiet out of season. It has an Iron Age hillfort and a 14th-century chapel dedicated to St Catherine, where spinsters once went to pray for a husband. It might look like a picture-postcard scene now but the village wasn't always so genteel. The *London Journal* recorded in 1725 that 'all the people of Abbotsbury, including the vicar, are thieves, smugglers and plunderers of wrecks'.

At the end of the village we turn left towards the Subtropical Gardens, an 18th-century garden containing plants from all over the world. On some evenings the gardens are illuminated. On down the hill we reach the beach car park, with toilets and a small shop. The ruin on the hill to our right is all that remains of Abbotsbury Castle, destroyed by fire in 1913.

We're now alongside Chesil Beach, which is in essence 18 miles of shingle stretching from West Bay to Portland. This is part of the Jurassic Coast, a UNESCO World Heritage Site. Here we are also on the South West Coast Path, the longest National Trail in the country at 630 miles.

*From here, by bike, there is the option to take Burton Road along the back of Chesil Beach. The plus side of this route means you avoid the significant hill and traffic back on the B3157; the minus is that the last section is unmade with stretches of loose shingle and very muddy in wet conditions – so you'll need to make your own decision. The tarmac runs out at the old coastguard cottages and deteriorates into a mile-long track. Rocket House in the foreground is presumably where the coastguard would have stored their life-saving rockets that fired lines to stricken ships.*

*The 'Unsuitable for Motor Vehicles' sign here is very reasonable, though a YouTube clip entitled 'Abbotsbury–Burton Road' features motorbikes enjoying its gravelly, damp glory. It's been a wet few weeks so the track is muddy with lots of big puddles and it's slow progress. Allan has a tough time pushing the tandem through the last 300 m of shingle to West Bexington Beach car park. We did this ride again at the end of a hot dry summer and it was a completely different experience.*

If you're driving, or worried about your bike and the potential walk, then it's back to the B3157 and turn left up the steep hill, then on for approximately 3 miles. There are fabulous views along this elevated stretch of road. Take the left turn opposite the Bull Inn to West Bexington, and join up with **the cyclists' only route** down at the beach car park.

The car park is right next to the beach, with toilets, an information board and map beside the pay machine. There's a memorial to Royal Marine Cpl Blain of the Special Boat Service. Shore fishing is popular here, with large numbers of cod caught in winter and plaice in spring. Views along the coast are fantastic. Behind the beach is one of DWT's few coastal nature reserves. The reedbed and scrub provide habitat for birds such as Cetti's warbler, reed bunting and linnet, dormice, water voles and great-crested newts.

We start up the hill, passing the Club House, with its deliciously fishy menu. It started life as a cafe in 1932 at a time when there were plans to develop the area into a premier seaside resort, 'Bexington-on-Sea'. Many bungalows and houses in the village date back to the 1930s. With an influx of visitors in mind, tennis courts and an outdoor pool were built just behind the beach. There are still some attractive chalets with small gardens overlooking the beach and sea. The intention was to hire these to holidaymakers as 'summer bungalows', but with the onset of WWII the ambitious scheme failed.

Near the top of this steep hill we pass the 16th-century Manor Hotel. On the corner is Tamarisk Farm, which manages 600 acres of mostly National Trust land. It was farming 'organically' before certification existed. The shop opens Tuesdays and Fridays or by appointment, but you can order online. Sea Spring Seeds are also based in West Bexington, a vegetable seed company run by gardeners for gardeners and renowned for their chillies including the Dorset Naga, one of the world's hottest varieties. Opposite Tamarisk Farm is an evocatively named lane Labour in Vain, leading to a farm of the same name.

We continue on and cross the B3157, through the village of Swyre, past the old school. The route carries straight on along Hazel Lane to meet a T-junction, but we turn right to visit Puncknowle (pronounced Punnel). The church here is adjacent to the manor house, which was occupied in the early 19th century by Colonel Shrapnel, inventor of the shell that bears his name. At the turn of the 20th century many residents were craftsmen, whose services made the community virtually self-sufficient. In 1903 there were two thatchers, a hurdle-maker, blacksmith, wheelwright, beehive-maker and dressmaker, as well as farmers, a rabbit dealer, three fish dealers, a shopkeeper and gardener. There is a 'Pub is the Hub' plaque on the wall

of the thatched Crown Inn, recognising its role in providing community services. A village shop operates within the pub, selling a range of local products, basic household provisions and newspapers.

Back at Hazel Lane we turn right signed Litton Cheney to meet a crossroads. We turn left and a little further on pass Modbury Farm Shop, with ducks and chickens roaming free in the yard.

We continue on to Burton Bradstock where you are spoiled for choice of potential eateries – two pubs, the popular Hive Beach Café at the NT car park, and the well-supported Village Farm Shop/PO. We take Cliff Road next to the garage, and overlooking the coast enjoy the quiet bench at the entrance to the tasteful Seaside Boarding House. This is still the SW Coast Path, with Chesil Beach below, but quite different geology, with crumbling 180-million-year-old sandstone cliffs, which are up to 40 m high.

We return to the garage, turn left, then take the third right at the Anchor Inn towards Shipton Gorge. Just before the S-bend and short rise to the New Inn, we turn right down Port Lane, then at the second crossroads go straight across NCN Route 2 and follow signs for Dorchester. We're skirting the lower slopes of the somewhat symmetrical Shipton Hill, so the lane does climb considerably to the A35. This is a busy junction, but we are going right in only 100 m. By bicycle we can walk along the right-hand verge. Then it's down the narrow lane signed Chilcombe.

After dropping down to what was once a cattle grid, the lane rises up, with spectacular views. Chilcombe means 'cold valley' and it can be rather windy here. Chilcombe Hill behind us is the site of yet another West Dorset hillfort – of which we are spoiled for choice. The hamlet ahead is partially hidden in woods. It has an interesting small church, which may be visited, but with respect as it's within the grounds of the pretty Manor House. The church has an unusual 17th-century wooden panel on the north wall directly opposite the door, inlaid with scenes depicting the Crucifixion. It once served as the church's reredos and is thought to be one of a tableau of three Christian iconographic carvings, the other two possibly portraying the birth and ascension of Christ.

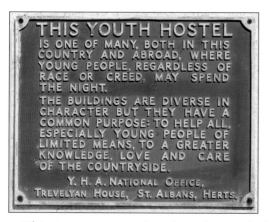

THIS YOUTH HOSTEL IS ONE OF MANY, BOTH IN THIS COUNTRY AND ABROAD, WHERE YOUNG PEOPLE, REGARDLESS OF RACE OR CREED, MAY SPEND THE NIGHT.

THE BUILDINGS ARE DIVERSE IN CHARACTER BUT THEY HAVE A COMMON PURPOSE: TO HELP ALL, ESPECIALLY YOUNG PEOPLE OF LIMITED MEANS, TO A GREATER KNOWLEDGE, LOVE AND CARE OF THE COUNTRYSIDE.

Y. H. A. NATIONAL OFFICE, TREVELYAN HOUSE, ST. ALBANS, HERTS.

Continuing on down the 1:7 lane brings us back to the crossroads just north of Puncknowle, where this time we go left towards Litton Cheney. Entering the village we pass the White Horse Inn, with the rather agricultural-looking Youth Hostel (a converted Dutch cheese and milk factory barn) down the lane to the right.

This is a pretty road with a chuggy little river and several houses with intriguing names, such as the Cheesehouse, Corn Bags and Faith House. We pause to admire the Old Mill with its collection of mill stones and water wheel. Up near the thatched bus shelter and Millennium stone are some cute wooden turnstiles on the path up to the church. It's a particularly pretty churchyard with great views over the Bride Valley.

We continue on towards Dorchester, ignoring White Way to our left with its steep climb up to the A35, and pass Hines Mead Lane to our right. The last property leaving Litton Cheney is Baglake Farm, with its tall, thatch-topped garden wall and 'secret' door, all of which look wonderful when the climbers are in full flower.

We reach the Long Barrow Hill junction, which gives away the presence of the 200-m-long 'bank barrow' high up to the left on Martin's Down. Archaeological finds in this area go back over 4500 years, with evidence of Anglo Saxon and Roman occupation. The barrow is easiest seen when driving along the A35, but we continue on into Long Bredy (pronounced Long Briddy). The first house on the left is Langebride House, the old rectory, with its imposing roadside wall topped with a beech hedge. It always looks its best in early summer, cloaked in alternate shades of green and copper leaves. The owners of the House open up the garden as part of the National Gardens Scheme, and in early spring the carpets of snowdrops, cyclamen, crocus and daffodils under the huge copper beech tree on the lawn, and in summer the lovely herbaceous borders, peonies and roses, fruit trees and a vegetable garden set within the old walls are a delight.

We bear right at the entrance to the 13th-century St Peter's Church, with its 'Living Churchyard' (meaning it's maintained in a way that provides optimum growing conditions for wild flowers), and descend to a junction, where we turn left signed Littlebredy. Heading out of Long Bredy you may get a glimpse of Kingston Russell House to the right, birthplace of Admiral Sir Thomas Masterman Hardy in 1769. The hamlet of Kingston Russell today is north of here, beyond the A35. A little further on is the far more obvious Bellamont House. We didn't know whether to be impressed or horrified by the extraordinary sight of gates with gilded ducks, beyond which are gate posts topped by elegant hounds, all guarding a generous sweep of lush green lawn leading to an old stately house. Except it's not! Bellamont House arrived on the scene in 1995. It took 8 months to build, using concrete blocks, and cost about £350,000. Described as a sham-Gothic eccentricity, it was featured in *Hello* magazine, *Country Life*, *Farmers Weekly* and *Architectural Digest*. Bellamont looks as if it's been part of the Dorset landscape for centuries. It certainly had us fooled. Next door is Bellamont Topiary, a family-run nursery.

We are about a mile from Littlebredy (pronounced Littlebriddy) and climb steadily towards the village, with wonderful views across the valley. Cycling these lanes is always a joy, but nothing can surpass that first time, a few years ago, when we were unaware of the delights in store. This beautiful village is a pleasure to visit and we can never cycle through without stopping. We pause beside the village green at the unusual six-sided shelter with seats. This is the oldest wooden bus shelter in Dorset and is kept in excellent condition, but only the school bus now stops. Inside, an oak tablet informs us that it was presented to the villagers on the occasion of Margaret and Philip Williams' silver wedding anniversary in 1933.

Allan wheels the tandem down a little path through St Michael and All Angels churchyard, and a notice invites visitors into the parkland but encourages a donation to the church and a local women's charity. This is all part of the private Bridehead House, home to seven generations of the Williams family, since it was purchased by Robert Williams in 1797. His French wife Jeanne Chasserau was famous locally for living to the age of 102. The current Sir Philip was High Sheriff of Dorset in 2016/17. The grounds are so gorgeous that the first time we came here I went back to re-read the notice to reassure myself we weren't trespassing.

There are large trout in the mirror-like lake, and taking centre stage is the cascading waterfall/weir, which featured in the *Broadchurch* TV series as a crime scene. It never seems crowded, despite its notoriety. This is the start of the River Bride, which flows for about 6.5 miles through open countryside until it enters the sea at Burton Bradstock beach. We take the lower exit from the gardens, along the stream, then the lane to the Walled Gardens. They used to supply fruit, vegetables and flowers to Bridehead House, and after volunteers restored the walls, old greenhouses and stone buildings, they are now open to visitors a couple of days a week during summer.

Back at the bus shelter, we head right past the old schoolhouse and forge on the left. We bear right following NCN Route 2 to the cricket ground. Even I don't mind stopping at this scenic natural bowl, with bordering sheep-filled fields and the attractive Bridehead House. Artist David Inshaw used this view as inspiration for his painting *The Cricket Game*. He was interviewed here by David Dimbleby for the 2005 TV series *A Picture of Britain*.

On a little further, we stop at the entrance to the Valley of Stones to admire some of the splendid long-horned cattle mentioned earlier in Abbotsbury. Continuing up the hill we have views to our left of Golden Cap, and a line of trees and bushes all leaning towards the northeast give their own ragged testimony of the prevailing winds at the head of this valley. We turn right and continue to the next T-junction with the Winterbourne Abbas to Portesham road. We turn right towards Portesham. After a short distance we come to the Portesham Hill Cross junction and we deviate right for a moment to look down on the Valley of Stones National Nature Reserve, with its large boulders littering the valley floor.

Back at Portesham Hill Cross junction, we go straight across towards the Hardy Monument. Despite being a landmark for miles around, when approaching from this direction it isn't visible until we are within about 300 m of the summit. It was erected in 1844 in memory of Vice-Admiral Sir Thomas Masterman Hardy, a commander at the Battle of Trafalgar in 1805 who served on the flagship *HMS Victory*. He became associated with the words 'Kiss me Hardy' or 'Kismet Hardy', whichever you prefer, because those were allegedly the dying words of Lord Nelson after he was felled by a French bullet. The monument here on Black Down Hill is 22 m (72 ft) high and intended to resemble a naval spyglass. The family chose the site to provide a landmark for shipping and it's been shown on navigational charts since 1846. Its foundation stone was laid by Hardy's three daughters on the 39th anniversary of the Battle of Trafalgar. The National Trust has owned it since

1938 and it's open to the public April to September, Wednesday to Sunday, but check the NT website first; 120 steps up a spiral stairway give visitors views across five counties.

Allan and I don't actually go up the monument, as we always worry about leaving the tandem. We lock it when we go into a teashop but still try to sit at a window table where it's visible. After 40 years of cycling, this is only our second tandem. It cost £2000 in 2003 and wasn't new then. A treasured member of the family, we would be distraught to lose it. Instead, we admire fantastic views of the Jurassic Coast, stretching over the Fleet, Chesil Beach and across to Portland. Southeast, Bronkham Down is littered with ancient burial mounds, with names such as Bowl Barrow, Pond Barrow and Saucer Barrow.

From here it's almost 2 miles whizzing downhill at up to 45.6 mph, before turning right at the T-junction into Martinstown, also known as Winterborne St Martin. Spotting a couple sitting outside the village shop drinking coffee, we stop to investigate and are pleased to discover that passing cyclists and walkers are given a warm welcome, inside and out. It's very pleasant sitting here enjoying coffee and chocolate brownies. There are also seats and an information board on the village green just ahead in front of the church, if you have a picnic.

Back on the tandem we continue through the village, ignoring a left turn to Dorchester and two left turns to Winterborne Monkton, then pedal up Gould's Hill. There's a layby at the top with views back over Maiden Castle hillfort. At the bottom of the hill we reach Upwey, with its famous Wishing Well. If you're not dining in the Tearooms and Water Gardens, entry to the well costs just £1. The well is a natural spring and it was long believed that its clear water held healing powers. In the early 20th century, Upwey was Weymouth's premier visitor attraction and horse-drawn charabancs transported holidaymakers from the seafront to the village. People would purchase a glass of well water from one of the local ladies who 'watched

the well'. After drinking most of it, they cast the dregs back into the well and made a wish. Upwey has also been popular with royalty. King George III drank his lucky water from a gold cup, kept at a nearby house for His Majesty's exclusive use, and which is alleged to have been used as one of the Ascot Gold Cups. Queen Charlotte (George III's wife) visited in 1798 and the Prince of Wales arrived in July 1923. To mark that occasion every school child was presented with a medal and given an afternoon's holiday.

In recent years there has been a well dressing event in May. This tradition has a long history in the Derbyshire Peak District but is something new for Dorset. A huge picture made from flowers and petals pressed into a clay base is carried at the head of a procession leading from Upwey village hall to the well. In 2018 this helped raise funds for provision of a defibrillator.

Retracing our steps slightly up Gould's Hill, we turn left towards Coryates along Friar Waddon Road, where we see brown hens scratching busily in fields. Further on, we pass a well-preserved thatched barn.

Ignoring the turn to Coryates we bear right on to Winters Lane, signed Little Waddon and Portesham, and enjoy cycling along this scenic lane with fields of sheep on either side. The views of Portland, Chesil Beach and the Fleet are beautiful. We stop to admire Waddon House. There's no long driveway shielding this ancient manor from the curiosity and cameras of passersby. In fact it sits directly on the side of the road and is very grand indeed, looking somewhat incongruous in such a rural setting.

All too soon we reach the main road back into Portesham, which locals refer to affectionately as 'Possum'. The farm shop on the main road to the left has a café and provisions for a picnic if needed. There's a small green opposite the pub, and we relax on a bench presented by the Possum Fes Wik Society in 2015. Possum Fes Wik was a week-long festival at the beginning of August between haymaking and harvest. It was discontinued on the outbreak of WWI, but in 1992 the festival was reborn as a fundraising event and over the

following years more than £60,000 was raised. Facing the green is Portesham House, former home of Thomas Masterman Hardy, Trafalgar hero and Lord Nelson's flag-captain. Close by is one of the few green telephone boxes in Dorset (there is another in Okeford Fitzpaine near Sturminster Newton). When phone boxes first appeared in the UK they encountered opposition in several rural areas because of their brash red appearance and some kiosks were repainted in more muted colours.

A ginger moggy strolls past but gives us a wide berth, despite my blandishments. Cats in Portesham seized the headlines in July 1936 with a story capturing the attention of media worldwide. The *Sydney Morning Herald* reported: 'The enterprising village of Portesham proposes to startle Britain with cat racing. 45 cats are in training. They will use an electric mouse and four traps. Betting facilities will be provided and an entrance fee of half-a-crown will be charged. It is suggested that a further development may be to use mice to chase electric cheese.' And it wasn't even April Fools' Day. The unlikely story was indeed fictitious and caused a minor uproar in the village.

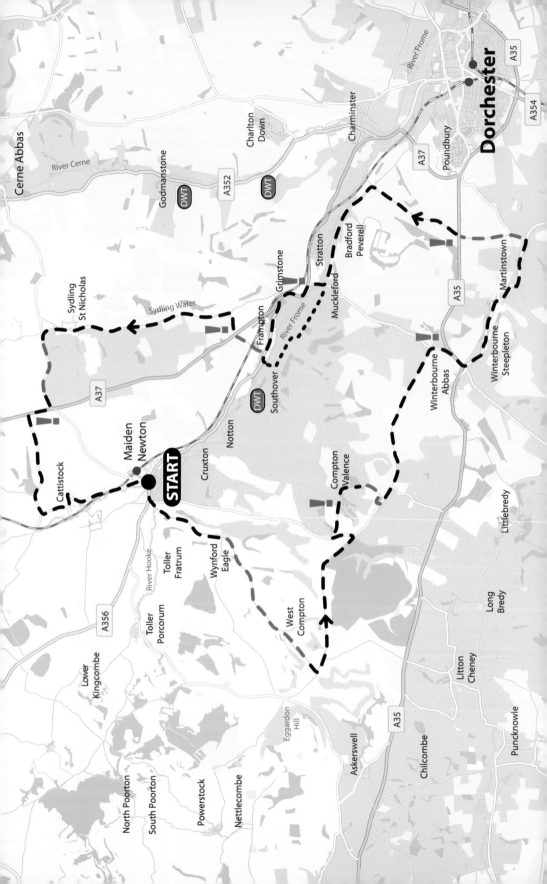

# Route 5 – Maiden Newton

*(visiting Wynford Eagle, Winterbourne Abbas, Martinstown, Frampton, Sydling St Nicholas and Cattistock)*

**Distance:** 26 miles (42 km)

**Hills:** 500 m elevation change, four significant hills

**OS map:** Explorer 117 and OL15

**Brief description:** This route winds through watery villages, over several bridges straddling the River Frome and past watercress beds. We look out for eagles, butterflies and hounds.

Before setting off from near the church and war memorial in Maiden Newton, we chat to a woman walking her dog who tells us she used to ride a tandem with her sister. She was always on the front and said it could be a problem when the one on the back tried to call the shots. Allan told her in our case it's *always* the one on the back who calls the shots. That's not true, of course. I didn't learn to ride a bike as a child and I still can't ride one now, so not being in control doesn't bother me. In fact, life as a stoker has many advantages. Protection from the worst of the elements comes high on this list. It's Allan who is directly in the firing line for the full force of lashing rain, freezing winds and hordes of nasty little black flies.

But today it's fine weather. Just down the road we pass the Old School on our left, with its clock and empty bell tower. We turn right at the village shop opposite remains of a 15th-century market cross onto the A356.

Just before the first bridge, on the right is a handsome old mill house and on the left a stone tower folly, all that remains of the old Castle Inn/ Hotel. Just on from here is a former Wesleyan chapel and bakery/grocers, both now private homes.

Leaving the village, we fork left signposted Wynford Eagle and over a hump-backed bridge at Tollerford Cross. Here we turn right along a tranquil lane and after about a mile see Wynford Eagle manor house (now Manor Farm). Built of honey-coloured stone in the centre of the hamlet, it is rather beautiful. Surmounting the three-storey porch is a stone eagle. A date of 1630 is carved under the bird, reinforcing an impression that it has been here a long time, but in fact this eagle is a Victorian successor to the original, whose headless remains were found in the gardens of the house not so long ago. We detour to look at pretty little St Laurence church,

which has a tympanum built into its west wall (*c* 1100) with two confronting wyverns.

Back at Manor Farm we continue towards West Compton (ignoring the left turn to that village) and tackle the steady climb up to Two Gates junction. Here we turn left past Eggardon Microwave Link Station. To our right we can clearly see the Hardy Monument and views stretching towards Purbeck. At the next junction we go left a short distance before turning right to drop down into Compton Valence and do a loop round the village. If you don't feel up to the extra hills you can continue on along Roman Road. We descend Church Hill Lane past St Thomas à Beckett Church into the tiny hamlet, which is well known for its display of snowdrops in February.

It's another climb back out of the village, and at the top we turn left towards Dorchester. The junction roundel informs us that this is a Roman Road, but it's not particularly straight. There's a lovely fast downhill stretch to the crossroads below Hillcrest Boarding Kennels, where we turn right and uphill again, past stacks of pallets, towards Winterbourne Abbas. Next it's a nasty junction just below the crest of a hill onto the A35, and we take our time pulling out. However, it's only 100 m downhill before we bear left signed Winterbourne Steepleton.

Winterbourne Abbas, off to the right, is worth a detour. The village has suffered occasional but significant flooding, even during summer. A self-help community group was formed in 2013 to undertake regular maintenance and clearing of vegetation from the South Winterbourne stream and there have been no significant problems since. The church is dedicated to St Mary and its oldest parts are 13th century, with a piscina (stone bowl) of that era, and a Jacobean gallery. The Coach and Horses Inn is now closed but dates from *c* 1814 when it was a coaching inn on the Dorchester to Bridport turnpike. Just west of the village alongside the A35 are The Nine Stones, probably the best example of a stone circle in Dorset. Also near the village are remains of ancient barrows and burial chambers.

We turn left at the pond onto the B3159 and immediately enter Winterbourne Steepleton, which takes its name from its stone church steeple, one of only three in Dorset. Apparently there are 49 round barrows within the parish boundary.

Steepleton Manor (now a luxury Residential Care Home) is an impressive-looking building but not nearly as old as its appearance might suggest. It was constructed from Portland stone in 1870, on the site of a 16th-century manor house.

Further on is Martinstown, also known as Winterborne St Martin. It's a fairly large, lively village with a post office store (and cafe area) and pub. It has a wonderfully detailed website, which, unlike so many, is kept up-to-date. At the end of the village we turn left towards Dorchester, but only for a short while before branching left and climbing steadily up Bats Lane. We cross over the A35, with the old radio station site to our right, then enjoy the long descent down Tilly Whim Lane (a name more associated with a quarry and caves at Durlston). Prince Charles's expanding Poundbury development is very obvious to our right, whereas there are miles of open fields to our left.

At Giles Cross there is often local produce for sale outside the farmhouse. Our route takes us left along the Frome Valley Trail into Bradford Peverell. This 16-mile walking and cycling route follows the river from Evershot to Dorchester (where it presently ends, though there are plans to extend it to Poole harbour). Around 400 people live in Bradford Peverell, but in years gone by the village was obviously a lot bigger because in 1836 a National School for 60 children was established. At the opposite end of the social scale and also during the 19th century, a finishing school for young ladies flourished here, primarily for the daughters of wealthy, aspirational Dorchester families. The Mill House is on the corner diagonally opposite the bus shelter, and the Old School was located next to the river down the lane to the right heading to the A37. However, we continue on, past the Old Dairy House on the left opposite a pretty section of the mill stream.

We approach Muckleford crossroads. *Motorists must detour here as the lane beyond Muckleford becomes private. Turning right at Muckleford crossroads takes you across two lovely little bridges over the River Frome and on to meet the A37. Go left, through Grimstone, passing the impressive viaduct (designed by*

*Isambard Kingdom Brunel), and left again onto the A356 into Frampton.*
*Just after the church, rejoin the route at the Millennium Green.*

On the tandem, we follow NCN Route 26 straight ahead through
Muckleford, which is such a small hamlet that if you blink you'll miss it.
Fortunately I wasn't blinking when we passed the rather fetching sign on a
cottage gate urging 'Beware of the Rabbit'. Not that I'm a fan of rabbits; it's
hard to be fond of a creature intent on decimating your vegetable garden.
Just after Littlewood Farm, NCN 26 turns sharp right over a cattle grid and
then immediately left towards Southover. However, it's worth a short detour
downhill to the right to appreciate the impressive stone Peacock Bridge
designed by Sir Christopher Wren.

Heading back towards Southover, smooth concrete gives way to a gravel track. At the end of this private road, opposite the Rose Garden, we turn right, away from NCN 26, and cycle over Samways (or Sandway) Bridge which spans the river. The simple yet beautiful white-painted wooden bridge is Listed, which makes periodic maintenance rather costly. Beyond is the Millennium Green, popular for picnics and paddling. We linger here for a while. Beside us is an abandoned length of rope, used the previous day in the annual cross-river tug-of-war competition (the losing team gets very wet).

My dad grew up in Frampton and although as a young man he moved to Broadstone, he always returned here for this event, one of the highlights of his year. The expanded village hall and events are well supported, and the amateur and professional theatre productions are very popular. Back on the bike, we turn right on the A356 and then left between the former alms houses and St Mary's Church.

A steep uphill stretch leads us to Long Ash Service Station on the A37. We cross straight over and take the lane down to a T-junction, where we turn left and pass through Magiston. There are a number of watercress beds on our right, feeding off the crystal-clear Sydling Water.

A few miles on we reach Sydling St Nicholas. Sydling Water flows down from the surrounding hills and divides into three streams as it passes through this pretty village, resulting in many properties being accessed by little bridges. The busy sound of running water is constant and we stop to admire the stream in the garden of Waterfall Cottage.

The village is home to the Greyhound Inn and at one time there was a second pub, intriguingly called the Hit or Miss. One explanation for this name is that sometimes the mail coach stopped here and sometimes it didn't; or it could have originated with the local hunt. The Hit or Miss is now a Grade II Listed house, overlooking the village green on East Street.

We walk to the church of St Nicholas, following a footpath sign to Breakheart Hill. The church is in a peaceful setting surrounded by fields. It's interesting to see the fireplace inside the porch where residents once held parish meetings. The 16th-century clock is one of the oldest in England. It is faceless but strikes the hours.

We pedal north out of the village towards Up Sydling, but at the next crossroads go left to Maiden Newton. It's a long climb to meet the A37 again. The route goes right for a few hundred metres, then left at Stagg's Folly junction down into Cattistock. This is a quietly scenic road overlooking the River Frome valley, with Charity Bottom to the right, Lankham Bottom to the left and Middle Hill between. Lankham Bottom Nature Reserve is managed by the Dorset branch of Butterfly Conservation. Adonis Blue, Grizzled Skipper, Dingy Skipper, Green Hairstreak, Brown Argus and Six-spot Burnet are some of the species that can be seen here.

At the bottom of the hill we turn left into Cattistock, which is well served with a post office shop, an interesting church and the Fox & Hounds Inn. Opposite the pub is the Savill Memorial Hall. Built in 1926, this was a rest centre during WWII for Dunkirk evacuees. Before D-Day the hall was used for entertaining American troops with dances and live shows. James Cagney is reputed to have performed here.

The village green has a well-equipped play area and used to host the annual Dorset Knob Throwing Festival, before it moved to Kingston Maurward because of its increasing popularity. 'Knob' biscuits have been made by Moores of Morcombelake since 1860, originally from leftover dough with added butter and sugar, hand-rolled and left to dry in the dying heat of the oven. It is thought the name comes from either the hand-sewn Dorset knob buttons made locally or their resemblance to door knobs.

We leave at the southern end of the village, where the braying of the kenneled hounds of Cattistock Hunt can often be heard. From its inception in the 1780s it was nicknamed 'the True Blue' because the majority of Dorset squires at that time were 'true blue' supporters of King George III, who often visited the area. After the pretty cricket ground, it's over the active Weymouth to Bristol railway line, and then the inactive spur to Bridport, which was decommissioned following the Beeching cuts. We're now back in Maiden Newton. At the offset crossroads we notice the old Toll House on our left, then turn right, back to the church.

I am more than ready for a rest, so we make our way to the churchyard in search of a quiet spot. It's not in great condition and the lettering is faint, but there's a seat here dedicated to Skip Squires, who died in 1990. Skip grew up in Maiden Newton during WWI. He was a farmer and operated a local milk round using a tractor and trailer. Village lads on their bikes were happy to deliver the bottles to doorsteps, so all Skip had to do was drive the tractor. The youngsters liked him and enjoyed helping out on the farm at weekends and in school holidays. Skip would hand out big mugs of coffee mid-morning, made with whole milk from his cows. This treat went down well, accompanied by thick slices of bread, hot from the oven of the nearby bakery and thickly spread with butter. Skip took an active part in village life and was especially involved in the church, where he was choirmaster and organist.

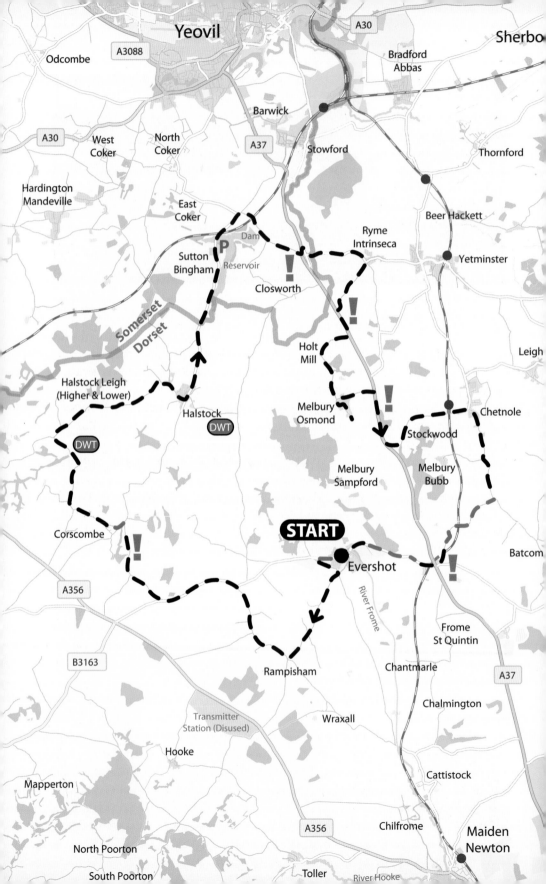

# Route 6 – Evershot

*(visiting Rampisham, Corscombe, Sutton Bingham, Melbury Osmond and Melbury Bubb)*

**Distance:** 25 miles (40 km)

**Hills:** 450 m elevation change, three significant hills

**OS map:** Explorer 117 and 129

**Brief description:** There's a real sense of old Dorset on this route, including a cart bridge in Rampisham, moats in Corscombe, a pilgrim route through Halstock and tiny churches. We pass the modest birthplace of Thomas Hardy's mother and feckless grandfather, and the awesome seat of the Earls of Ilchester.

From Evershot we proceed up West Hill past the church, turn left at the top towards Cattistock, and then right downhill towards Rampisham. The large aerial on Rampisham Down is some way off on the ridge directly ahead. There used to be 26 pylons here, clearly visible from any high point in West Dorset, and the site was one of the main transmitters of the BBC World Service in Europe, but it was closed in 2011. Natural England is restoring the land to a wildlife habitat, and the remaining pylon has become a nesting platform for peregrine falcons.

We enjoy the speedy descent of Broom Hill, but pause to admire remains of an old wayside cross at Broomhill Farm. Then it's on down into Rampisham (known locally as Ransom), past the picturesque thatched and whitewashed old post office. Across the small ford (dry today, though the depth gauge

indicates it can reach 6 ft), we pause on the new bridge to admire an old cart bridge to our left. The stonework is romantically overgrown, but it's still used as a bridleway.

The former Tiger's Head Inn is across the junction. This burnt down in the early 20th century and was replaced by a much larger building, which remained as a pub until the early 1990s. It's now a private house and over the doorway is carved 'REBUILT 1915'. We turn right here and enjoy the gentle rise out of the village. On our right is the old school, with at least one famous past scholar – Francis Glisson (1597–1677). Francis was schooled in Rampisham and went on to be Professor Regius of Cambridge University for 40 years and a founder member of the Royal Society in London. He wrote learned papers on rickets (partly observed in Dorset) and anatomy of the liver.

After part-timbered Rose Cottage and a timber yard in Uphall, we reach a T-junction at Benville Bridge. This is one of several Dorset bridges adorned with a plaque issuing the same stern warning: 'Any person wilfully injuring any part of this County bridge will be guilty of felony and upon conviction liable to be transported for life. By the Court. T. FOOKS'. These plaques are believed to date from the late 1820s, when sentencing was harsh and at least 50 different crimes were classified as capital offences. Other misdemeanors carrying the death penalty were setting fire to a heap of hay, stealing from a shipwreck, going out at night with a blackened face and impersonating a Chelsea Pensioner. A few hundred metres beyond the bridge is one of Dorset's four red signposts (see Routes 1 and 8 for others). Like the rest it has white lettering on its red fingers, but as it's on a small traffic island the fingers are often missing. Corscombe village website suggests this Red Post is haunted by a post of soldiers that died here, and it should not be passed at night.

At the T-junction we turn left signed Beaminster. Before the top of the hill we come to Benville Farm and take the right turn signed Corscombe. The large private house immediately on our right is Benville Manor, Grade II* Listed, with a separate moat in its grounds. At the next T-junction we turn

right and enjoy a fast, narrow descent to the 400-year old Fox Inn. Diagonally opposite is Corscombe Court, one of Dorset's oldest buildings (13th century). It's another property with a moat (this time visible from the road), and there's also a 15th-century tithe barn that was used by Sherborne Abbey monks, just visible through gates across the yard.

*Corscombe Court.*

We start heading up Court Hill, bear right along the much flatter Court Lane, then down Fudge Hill into the main part of the village. Many fields and farms in the area have American names because of the village's connection with Thomas Hollis (born 1720) whose uncle was the main benefactor of Harvard University. Thomas only spent 4 years in Corscombe but was responsible for undertaking extensive repairs to the church. Just south of here near Beckham's Coppice are some large stones, believed to be the remains of a chambered long barrow and known locally as the Devil's (or Granny's) Armchair. During the 18th and 19th centuries many Corscombe inhabitants were involved in smuggling. Witchcraft and ghost stories are also plentiful. Electricity only arrived in 1951 and mains water in 1953. Towards the middle

of the village is Pitts Farm, built around 1760. At one time it was Corscombe's second public house (the George Inn), which closed in about 1885 when it became a bakery (now also closed).

We pedal out of the village and wind our way past Bracketts Coppice, originally rough grassland (Birch Common) and now a DWT nature reserve with long-horn cattle grazing on it. On into Halstock Leigh, then to Halstock with its legend of Saint Juthware, a beautiful and devout Saxon woman who carried her head to the church altar after she was beheaded by her brother Bana. The former Quiet Woman pub is now a private house doing B&B, but their sign and glazed front door depict the history. Halstock and Corscombe lie on the route of the ancient Harrow Way or Old Way, which dates to 600–450 BC though it was probably in existence even earlier (since the Stone Age). It ran from Seaton (Devon) to Dover, and its eastern end from Winchester to Canterbury became known as the Pilgrims' Way. It is sometimes described as the 'oldest road in Britain' and is possibly associated with ancient tin trading.

We head north past the well-stocked community shop and Internet café and soon reach Sutton Bingham reservoir, where we stop for elevenses. Sutton Bingham shouldn't really be mentioned in this book because it lies just over the border in Somerset, but it's a beautiful spot and an ideal place to have a break. There's fishing (from the bank or a boat) and a sailing club, so invariably something interesting to watch; public toilets too are always a bonus.

Back on the tandem, we cycle over the causeway, with water on either side, and under a railway bridge, turning right after half a mile towards Netherton and Closworth. Goose Slade Farm Shop and Tea Rooms is on our left. On the run-up to Christmas there are lots of geese being fattened up on this organic farm, which has been run by the same family since 1923.

On under Netherton railway bridge, we pass water works below the reservoir dam. Just up the next small hill is a post box on an island junction, and the lane to the right has a permanent sign warning of potholes – has the council given up? Continuing on, we need to cross over the A37 heading for Ryme Intrinseca. Bikes can go straight across the A37 on the cycle path. *Cars must go left at this junction, before turning immediately right in front of Hamish's Farm Shop and Café and then left into Ryme.*

Before 1102 this village was in Somerset. 'Ryme' comes from Old English *Rima* meaning edge or border and 'Intrinseca' means 'lying within the bounds'. There was once a Manor of Ryme Extrinseca in Long Bredy and Langton Herring. The Prince of Wales' feathers on the end wall of the Post House and the name Prince's Farm remind us that the village was once the property of the Duchy of Cornwall. The 13th-century church is one of only two in England dedicated to St Hyppolyte. In the church is an alms dish that went missing in 1873 and found its way back to Dorset 65 years later.

At the edge of the village we turn right signed Melbury Osmond and immediately right again signed Unsuitable for Heavy Vehicles. We cross a small tributary of the River Yeo. There's a field of solar panels to our left as we meet the A37 again. Here we go left for just 500 m, then turn right to Holt Mill. The Potting Shed on our right is a mix of nursery, eatery and wellness retreat, a 'special place to relax, unwind & be inspired' in its pretty garden.

On down the lane we pass some Ilchester Estate offices. A local told us that doors painted blue denote properties belonging to the Estate. Further on is tastefully converted Holt Mill. Round the corner and up over the hill, thatched Glebe Cottage has an interesting mix of wooden and stone mullion windows. The driveway gate is 'Dorset' style – predominantly wooden framed with horizontal metal bars.

At the T-junction we turn right to pass the Old School House, still with its original bell. Round the corner is St Osmund's Church. Past clergy include the Rev John Biddell, who after his death in 1732 was described as 'a person of such universal goodness that 'tis difficult to single out any virtue in which he was more particularly eminent'. Equally virtuous was parishioner Mary Ainslie (died 1757) whose husband of 21 years 'never saw her once ruffled with anger or heard her utter a peevish word'. Various family names such as Childs, Groves and Pitcher were ubiquitous over the years. Alfred John Pitcher (1846–1930) lies beneath a headstone declaring that he was 'Born in Sin'. Harry Pitcher was the last of his name to live in Melbury Osmond and he moved to Leigh after WWII. I was dismayed to discover that a namesake of ours – James Winter – broke into the village shop in 1800 and was subsequently hanged at Dorchester Prison!

Inside the church is a framed copy of Thomas Hardy's parents' marriage certificate. Hardy's maternal grandparents grew up in Melbury Osmond and his grandmother Betty Swetman came from a respectable family of yeoman farmers. A clever girl, love proved her undoing when she fell for a young chap named George Hand. Father Swetman strongly disapproved of his daughter's suitor, possibly because Betty was 8 months pregnant when the couple married. George was also overly fond of the bottle and described as a gardener and shepherd by trade, but only 'when sober'. Betty's father disinherited her, and when George died she was left destitute with seven young children. Her fifth child, a daughter named Jemima, fell in love with a stonemason and builder from Higher Bockhampton. History repeated itself and, like her mother, Jemima walked down the aisle heavily pregnant. She gave birth to

a son, Thomas Hardy. He was to become one of the greatest novelists and poets in English literary history. As a child, Jemima lived in No. 1 Barton Hill Cottages behind the church. (*There is some parking space near the church, so motorists wishing to stroll through Melbury Park should leave their car here.*)

Just down the lane is the Old Post House, then an information board in a lovely stone feature before the ford. There's a small packhorse bridge and a long raised pavement to keep your feet (and wheels) dry. The water level is low, but we push the tandem over the bridge because cobbles under the water hide gaps that could catch the wheel and have us off. On holiday in Exmoor we encountered a ford Allan didn't like the look of for similar reasons, and from the safety of the bridge we watched a cyclist pedal into the water and promptly fall off his bike. Fortunately he was unhurt, but Allan couldn't help feeling a bit smug.

Ahead on the left are two thatched properties separated by a bridleway. Monmouth Cottage, home of Hardy's great grandparents, is one of numerous Dorset houses where the Duke of Monmouth (Charles II's eldest illegitimate son) is supposed to have taken refuge – a legend that Hardy wove into his short story *The Duke's Reappearance*. Walnut Tree Cottage has a plaque stating 'This is a Wildlife Friendly Garden'. The DWT operates a scheme whereby people are entitled to a plaque if they can provide photographic evidence of at least six appropriate items in their garden; these include a pond, compost heap, native tree, shrubbery with berries, bat box, and log pile or decaying tree stump.

We cycle on to Townsend Farm Dairy, aptly named as vehicles and cycles are not permitted any further (mechanically operated gates bar all motorists and cyclists except those entitled to enter). Here an estate worker with a young spaniel called Percy explained that around 20 cycling permits are issued at any time to residents of Evershot and Melbury Osmond only. *If you have time it's an interesting and very enjoyable walk through Melbury Park, either circular or through to Evershot. However, there is ample parking at the Evershot end, which we'll pass later so the walk is easier from that end.* Melbury Sampford parish seems to comprise of Melbury House, estate and deer park. The house was rebuilt in 1530 by Sir Giles Strangways, Henry VIII's Dorset Commissioner for the Dissolution of the Monasteries.

Deer parks originated in medieval times and were once scattered throughout Dorset. They supplied a valuable source of fresh meat and conferred status on those who owned them, but most had a short life as they were expensive to maintain. Sherborne, Melbury and Stock Gaylard estates are the only Dorset parks still grazed by fallow deer today.

Melbury Park is part of Ilchester Estates. Capability Brown landscaped the 900-acre park in the 18th century, but one remarkable tree existed here long before that. Known as Billy Wilkins (after William Wilkins, an estate manager in the 17th century), this gnarled old oak has an extraordinary girth of over 11 m. There are many more magnificent trees here, including other great oaks, limes and an avenue of sycamores.

Melbury House has been in the Strangways family for more than 500 years and was the seat of the Earls of Ilchester until 1964. Thomas Hardy called it King's Hintock Court in some of his stories. Photography pioneer Henry Fox Talbot was born here. Its tower has a room with views in five directions, apparently extending as far as the Mendips and Quantock Hills. Next to the house is St Mary's Chapel, once the parish church of the lost village of Melbury Sampford, but as with the house it is generally kept private. During WWII and prior to D-Day, Melbury House and Park were occupied by American Forces.

Retracing our steps from Townsend Farm Diary, past the Old School again, we bear right at the T-junction towards the A37. First though we pass a bus shelter on our right, erected by public subscription to commemorate the coronation of Queen Elizabeth II in June1953. The first concrete block shelter was moved from its original site and rebuilt here in stone in 1990.

Further on, we turn right onto the A37 for about 600 m, past the Sheaf of Arrows pub (formerly the Rest and Welcome Inn), then take a quiet lane on the left to Stockwood. An Historic Church sign leads us to St Edwold's, Dorset's smallest church at around 9×4 m and the second smallest church in England. It's maintained by the Churches Conservation Trust. Although still consecrated, services are rarely held here, but one is due the following week on St Edwold's Feast Day, 29 August. This being my birthday, I feel an unfamiliar affinity with a saintly figure. There is seating for probably fewer than 30 people and the church is plain, with a stone floor, wooden chairs and leaded windows.

Back on route we cycle over a bridge with lonely looking Chetnole station on our left. The railway here is a branch line between Westbury and Weymouth, opened in 1857 and now part of the Bristol to Weymouth 'Heart of Wessex' line. Chetnole, nearby Yetminster and Thornford are the only three 'request stop' stations in Dorset. Very few people use them and passengers

must flag the train down like a bus. Rather surprisingly there are around 150 such stations in Britain (about 6% of all stations). Chetnole is mentioned/covered in Route 7, so at the T-junction we turn right and scoot on towards the intriguingly named Hell Corner. There is another Hell Corner in Dorset in the east of the county near Chalbury, situated between Holt and Horton.

The hamlet of Melbury Bubb is down the lane to the right, with its Jacobean manor house and walled garden. In Hardy's *The Woodlanders* it is known as Little Hintock and described as 'such a small place that, as a town gentleman, you'd need to have a candle and lantern to find it if ye don't know where 'tis'. St Mary's Church is still lit by oil lamps and has some medieval stained-glass windows and an elaborate font carved out of the column of an upturned Saxon cross depicting intertwined hunting animals upside-down. A multi-fuel stove and two coal scuttles lend a cosy, homely touch to the church. At this point it is just a 400-m walk over Bubb Down to St Edwold's which we visited earlier.

Back at Hell Corner we turn right towards Batcombe, then right towards Evershot up a sunken lane. Across the A37 one last time, we go over the railway line which emerges from the Evershot tunnel where Evershot station used to be, through Holywell, and back up (and down) into Evershot, the second highest village in Dorset at approximately 175 m (574 ft) above sea-level (Ashmore is the highest at 210 m (700 ft)). There's a small triangular grass area with an interesting stone seat made of three standing stones known as the Three Dumb Sisters. Local legend has it that these were three sisters turned to stone for dancing on the Sabbath. Away up the lane to the right is the southern entrance to Melbury Park, again with mechanically operated gates, this time guarded by two stone lions.

In the village I notice an attractive sign with an image of a delivery chap riding his bicycle, front basket piled high with cottage loaves. We go in search of the bakery and can't resist buying a couple of iced custard slices. Allan makes all our bread and cakes but so far hasn't attempted a custard slice. There's been a bakery in Evershot since 1857. The renowned Summer Lodge Country House Hotel was built as a dower house by Henry Fox-Strangways, 2nd Earl of Ilchester, in 1798. A dower house is a property made available to a widow (dowager) on the death of her husband. It became a hotel in 1979.

The Acorn Inn is proud of its literary associations. In Hardy's novel *Tess of the D'Urbervilles*, Evershot is referred to as Evershed and the Acorn Inn as the Sow and Acorn. This former 16th-century coaching inn was originally the King's Arms. It had stiff competition as there were once six pubs in the village. No wonder the records of a long-ago police constable lists 'drunk and disorderly' as the most frequent crime in the village. The landlord of the

Acorn used to brew his own ales with water drawn from the source of the River Frome, accessible just behind the church (with a good information board). The river probably saved Evershot in 1865, when a fire raged through the village, destroying 14 cottages plus other buildings. £70 (the equivalent of about £3000 today) was quickly raised to help the 100 homeless residents. Thankfully there was no loss of life or injury, but somewhat grimly the *Western Gazette* (6 October 1865) reported that carpets, blankets and a butt of cider had been plundered from the rescued items.

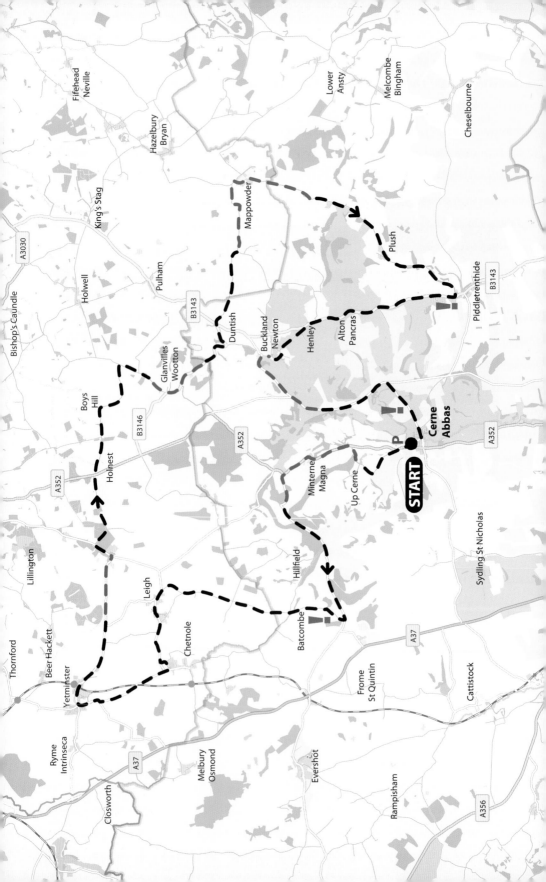

# Route 7 – Cerne Abbas

*(visiting Batcombe, Leigh, Mappowder, Piddletrenthide and Buckland Newton)*

**Distance:** 37 miles (59 km)

**Hills:** 630 m elevation change, two significant hills

**OS map:** Explorer 117 and 129

**Brief description:** We visit one of the most desirable villages in Britain, stop for views by a cross in the hedge and are intrigued by the history of a lost miz-maze. We Wriggle and Piddle, stopping at blue plaques, and talk to some church crawlers.

From the village hall car park we head north, up past the Cerne Giant viewpoint. The 55-m-high giant is brazenly male and arrogantly naked, carved into the chalk hillside. His origins are uncertain; they could be Roman or perhaps much more recent. On 1 November 2013 the giant sported a magnificent grass moustache in support of 'Movember', which raises awareness of prostate and testicular cancer. The addition of facial hair made him look a lot jollier and somewhat diverted attention from his most obvious physical attribute.

Turning right onto the A352, we pass Casterbridge Manor Care Home, which originally opened in 1837 as the Cerne Union Workhouse, and went on to be a boys' remand home and then a youth hostel. We soon bear left to loop through Up Cerne, a beautiful village with a Grade II* Listed 17th-century manor house and large lake. You know you are in rather a unique village because even the signs are courteous: 'Kindly keep all dogs on leash'. There are only seven properties here, mostly of flint and stone. The gabled manor house was built using stone from the remains of Cerne Abbey and was given to Sir Walter Raleigh by Elizabeth I. We stop to admire the pretty cottages and peer into the tiny chalk stream, where we once spotted a crayfish. Maps suggest the River Cerne rises just north of here, but the main stream seems to start a little higher up the valley at Minterne Magna.

From here it's quite a climb back to the A352 where we turn left, past Minterne Parva and through Minterne Magna. The manor house isn't open to the public but the gardens generally are and they're worth a visit, with at least a mile of peaceful woodland to explore, through beautiful parkland and round a lake. If time is short, you can briefly appreciate the lake setting from near the entrance.

We bear left to Batcombe, and after a steady rise there is a lovely flat road along the ridge. It's pleasant cycling and we're probably taking it a bit too easy because we're suddenly overtaken by a couple of young chaps on bikes, who pronounce the tandem as 'awesome'. Their bulky panniers suggest they are probably camping. As OAP cyclists we're used to being overtaken by fit young fellows but that doesn't mean we like it. We pass a right turn to Hilfield, whose manor is a former Victorian hunting lodge. Hilfield Friary is now a retreat centre, offering events and talks and welcoming people from all over the world. It was the first community in Britain to be presented with an Eco Church Gold Award, reflecting on the importance of looking after the environment as an expression of faith.

After a few hundred metres there's a stone pillar fenced off, almost hidden in the hedge on the right. It's about 1m tall and people have left coins on it, which strikes me as odd. It's known locally as the Cross-in-Hand (or Cross and Hand), because a cross once surmounted it and apparently the outline of a hand is still discernable, though we couldn't see it. Legend suggests this stone marks the spot where a murderer lies buried, having first sold his soul to the devil. Hardy used the pillar in his novel *Tess of the D'Urbervilles* in a scene in which Alec d'Urberville instructs Tess to 'put your hand upon that stone hand, and swear that you will never tempt me – by your charms or ways'. The pillar also features in Hardy's poem *The Lost Pyx*. Here on Batcombe Hill we are rewarded by terrific views stretching as far as the Mendips. We can even see Alfred's Tower near Stourhead Gardens in Wiltshire almost 30 miles away.

We take the next right and drop off the ridge towards Batcombe, stopping to visit the rather plain but charming church of St Mary Magdalene with its impressive tower. A caring attitude for those less fortunate is demonstrated by a notice that reads: 'Blankets for visiting wayfarers may be found under a

rear pew'. If it's anything like our village church, on chilly Sundays members of the congregation might appreciate a snuggly blanket too.

The Minterne family were lords of the manor in Batcombe between the 16th and 18th centuries and Newlands Farm further down the valley was the manor house. The original ashlar ham-stone archway (*c* 1622) predates the Georgian house that stands here today. In one of Dorset's more curious tales, a local squire known as Conjuring Minterne rode his horse off Batcombe Hill and knocked one of the pinnacles off the church tower. Although he dabbled in magic and was regarded with a great deal of fear and superstition, a 'conjurer' was an important character in a Dorset village and was generally of good reputation. Allegedly gifted with supernatural powers which were exercised for good, his incantations and ceremonies were believed to have cured many sicknesses.

We're really getting a move on along this road and suddenly we catch a glimpse of those two cyclists not far ahead. Allan and I haven't ridden a tandem for 40 years without developing a fine-tuned telepathy. He pushes down hard on the pedals and I follow suit. Stealthily we gain on the unsuspecting lads. We bear right at the next junction and head for Leigh (pronounced Lye), best known for its miz-maze. Unlike usual mazes, a miz-maze has no junctions or crossings and is more like a rope laid out neatly on the ground. There are very few of these turf mazes left in the country and its remains are now barely visible. It may have been used in rituals, as this corner of Leigh Common is also known as Witches' Corner. We lose speed while I'm dithering about whether or not I want to look for the miz-maze and by the time I've decided against, all is lost and we've missed a rare opportunity to whizz triumphantly past a couple of young 'uns. They disappear over the horizon, never to be seen again.

At the well-preserved stone cross we head left to Chetnole. Just before the village and on a bend, cyclists can investigate the aptly named Deep Ford Lane and then turn right to Hamlet and Yetminster. The delightfully named River Wriggle cuts through here, and the associated footbridge is well raised up to cope with flooding. ***There are signs at either end saying Unsuitable For Motorists, who should therefore continue to the next*** *junction at Chetnole Inn and turn right.* Across the playing field from the ford is Chetnole House. To its right is an impressive outbuilding with a large dovecote built into the gable end.

At Yetminster Cross Roads junction we again turn right, signed Leigh. Ahead is the Old School Gallery and Café, with a blue plaque on the wall commemorating 17th-century scientist Sir Robert Boyle (pioneer of modern chemistry, best known for Boyle's Law). He left money in trust for the education of 20 poor boys from Yetminster, Leigh and Chetnole, and the school operated between 1711 and 1945.

Near the church there is another blue plaque at Upbury Farm, to Benjamin Jesty, a farmer who lived in the village. Jesty discovered the vaccination for smallpox in 1774 after deliberately infecting his wife and two eldest sons with cowpox to prevent them getting smallpox; however, he didn't publicise his findings, so credit and financial reward went to Edward Jenner in 1796. His portrait hangs in the Dorset County Museum and his gravestone lies in Worth Matravers (where he later lived).

Yetminster is an attractive village, with honey-coloured limestone houses perhaps more indicative of nearby Somerset. The clock on the church is faceless, but it makes up for it by playing the National Anthem every three hours, at 12, 3, 6 and 9 o'clock. The chimes were installed in 1897 to celebrate Queen Victoria's Diamond Jubilee. Yetminster Fair can trace its origins back to 1300. The event lapsed in the 19th century but was revived and is now held on the second Saturday in July. It is unlikely anyone visiting the fair nowadays will walk away with a prize pig, but in 1911 that was exactly what happened. There was a competition in which a man had to sing a song while holding a piglet in his arms. The singer who most successfully drowned out the pig's squealing was voted the winner and got to take it home.

We head out of the village over the railway towards Leigh, but after a mile or so bear left towards Longburton. At Bailey Ridge junction we turn left, and shortly after go right towards Holnest. This is a rather strung-out community. We cross the A352, heading towards Boys Hill. On our left is Rylands Farm, part of the Future Roots enterprise, providing a therapeutic environment for young people with learning difficulties and who are interested in farming and the countryside.

Allan is just saying how lovely and quiet this lane is when we hear the rumble of a tractor coming up behind us. Allan immediately starts looking for somewhere to pull over and let the driver overtake because the noise of a tractor in hot pursuit sounds quite menacing. Tractors are big these days and often take up the width of a country lane. And they seem to travel much faster than they used to. Gone are the days when we could keep up with one and pedal for miles in its slipstream. Thirty years ago while on holiday in Somerset we cycled behind a tractor for 6 miles, all the way from Dunster to Watchet.

Just before the end of this lane is Round Chimneys Farm. This former mansion once owned by the first Sir Winston Churchill (1620–88) was also the home of his son John, 1st Duke of Marlborough, and to the highwayman John Clavell. The round chimneys can be seen from the lane.

Next stop is Glanvilles Wootton. We pass the war memorial and village coat of arms, the latter explaining how the village name derives from Henry de Glanville (*c* 1210) and *wootton* meaning a glade in the woods.

We push the tandem along a narrow shady path signed 'To the Church on foot only'. There is an entrance on the road down Locks Lane as well but we are rather fond of this route. St Mary's is quietly situated and there is a splendid seat with the inscription 'In Loving Memory of Chris Knapman 2/1/1951–15/2/1997. Always in our Hearts'. One time we visited, a dog tied to this bench was dozing peacefully beside a bowl of water. I'm rather a wuss where dogs are concerned, probably because they like chasing bikes, but even I could see that this one was entirely unthreatening. He watched us enjoying our tea and biscuits and I did my best to ignore his hopeful expression. We chatted to the dog's owner, who turned out to be a member of the Church Recorder Group affiliated to NADFAS (the National Association of Decorative and Fine Arts Societies). This group was spending several weeks surveying the textiles, paintings, woodwork, memorials and so on inside the church, their findings to be recorded in an illustrated book and presented to St Mary's. Some encaustic floor tiles in the chantry depict the legend of the killing of King Henry III's protected white stag. Many other Dorset churches have been surveyed in recent years, including Beaminster, Burton Bradstock and Chideock. It was time for us to go and the dog, a Labradoodle named Banjo, managed to incorporate sad bewilderment into his expectant gaze. Allan and I finally gave in and parted with one biscuit.

Carrying on towards Buckland Newton, we bear left towards Duntish, until Duntish Corner. Here we pass a lovely gate at the entrance to Castle Hill and Duntish Court. We continue left to the B3143.

At this junction we go left and then right to reach Mappowder, turning right and right again towards the church. The name of the village may derive from the Old English *mapluldor* meaning maple tree.

One day at Mappowder church, we realised for once we didn't have the place to ourselves. A group of 'church crawlers' from Sherborne U3A was visiting (the poet John Betjeman, who loved country churches and often visited them on his bicycle, created the term 'church crawling'). They told us that every month they explored a couple of Dorset churches, always finishing with a pub lunch. From the churchyard we look east over the back of Mappowder Court, beyond which is Bulbarrow Hill as it drops towards Ansty. The original and more substantial manor house was built here in the 16th century by the Coker family, who reputedly made their fortune from the slave trade. The entrance pillars were topped with sculptured negro (Blackamore) busts, celebrating the importance of the family and their involvement with this dreadful business. Something similar is prominent on the Coker family crest and coat of arms. The Cokers left the house in 1610 and eventually sold it and the estate in 1745 due to debts. It was bought by the Hon. John Spencer, whose descendants became the Earls Spencer and one of their daughters was Princess Diana. The present house looks very different at the front (rendered) compared to the back (grey stone).

We continue on and then drop into Plush, along a short but slightly unnerving sunken section of the lane – dark even in daylight. We bear left just before the Brace of Pheasants and the intriguingly named Plush Bottom house. Allan and I went to the Brace (our favourite pub) for dinner with friends in 1975 on our first wedding anniversary, and we've celebrated with the same friends every year since on their wedding anniversary and ours.

Further on we pass the cricket ground and eventually enjoy the 1:5 descent to the Poachers Inn at Piddletrenthide, where we turn right. To visit the church we take the second left into Church Lane. Past the stream and Mill Cottage, with its old mill stone and garden features, we come to All Saints. Over the many years we've cycled through this village we've become rather fond of the beautiful seat in the churchyard dedicated to Kathleen Jakeman (1925–80): 'In thankfulness for the happiness she gave'. Kathleen met her future husband George in Reading, when her father was manager of Reading Football Club. They married in 1947 and moved to Piddletrenthide in 1951, where George worked on the Wightman family farm. Kathleen entered enthusiastically into every aspect of village life and helped compile the hugely successful *Piddle Valley Cook Book* in 1978. This raised funds for All Saints, where George was churchwarden for 25 years. I remember how popular the cookery book was when I worked in the library, and even now Dorset Library HQ still has a copy. There are some great recipes, such as Una's Mother's Flaky pastry, Rumble Thumps and Piddle Potage. Leaving the churchyard, round to the right we notice a sign outside a house for honey and a book of village memories for sale.

Back on route we continue up the Piddle valley to Alton Pancras, source of the River Piddle. *Awultune* is Saxon for settlement at a spring and Pancras refers to the saint. The church organ was originally from a fairground, so it has a different tone to most. Opposite the church entrance is Burnt House Bottom, a valley with an ancient field system and strip lynchets. There is a particularly detailed and well-illustrated information board, and part way up the hill a seat commemorates all the people who lived in the village in 2000.

We head on up the valley, and just after Dorset Badger Watch and Henley Hillbillies turn left through Henley and on down to the Gaggle of Geese pub in Buckland Newton. Going left we weave round to visit the church. While enjoying a peaceful view of surrounding fields, we speculate on two horses, each in its own field and ignoring the other. Don't they get on, we wonder? A snug seat in the churchyard is tempting, placed in memory of Kit and Izzy Ward, a somewhat eccentric couple who lived in the village. Kit was an old Etonian and retired army colonel, often seen wearing shorts held up with string and who tied wire mesh onto the windscreen of his car to stop stones chipping the glass. Izzy would only grow clematis in her garden, absolutely nothing else unless it could be used to hang more clematis on. To the north of the church and close to the boundary hedge is a poignant memorial in the form of a small stone pillar with four panels. It commemorates 13 local children (the youngest aged 10 months) and one adult who died in an epidemic of either cholera or typhoid in 1858 – the year was known nationally as 'The Year of the Great Stink'. We turn right away from the church, then immediately bear left up to Knapps Hill junction, where we turn left. It's rather steep at first but levels out along Ridge Hill, with great views either side.

At Revels Hill junction we again go left signed Cerne Abbas, past Giant's Head Caravan Park, and then at Alton Drove junction turn right down the steep hill back into Cerne Abbas. We're always happy to cycle 'down' here rather than up. In Abbey Street, opposite the Tudor Pitch Market, we have a rest in Squibb Garden adjoining the church. There are several seats here and we make our choice according to whether we prefer sunshine or shade. It's a well-tended garden with flowering shrubs, wild strawberries and fruit trees. A politely worded request reads 'Please help yourself to windfalls. Apples on trees are juiced and sold in aid of the church'. We usually have the place to ourselves, although one day someone asked if we had come to do the gardening! Our view is enlivened by some pied wagtails hunting for insects

on the steep stone tiles of a nearby house. Further along at the end of Abbey Street is a pretty pond.

Journalist Kate Adie lives in the village and I often wonder which of the lovely houses belongs to her. In 2008 Cerne Abbas was chosen as Britain's

most desirable village by estate agent Savills, and homes here tend to sell for around 26% more than the Dorset average. Little remains of the 10th-century Benedictine abbey it grew up around, but there is a rich diversity of historic architecture. The high percentage of Listed buildings is obviously helping to protect it from development, and the community seems strong with a well-supported post office shop and two pubs. It appears in Thomas Hardy's novels as Abbot's-Cernel.

On the tandem again, it's a short ride back to the village hall.

# Route 8 – Puddletown

*(visiting Tolpuddle, the Winterbornes and Bulbarrow)*

**Distance:** 37 miles (60 km)

**Hills:** 680 m elevation change, one significant hill

**OS map:** Explorer 117

**Brief description:** This is a tour with several beautifully situated historic manor houses and a remote 12th-century thatched chapel. Pretty villages follow the chalk streams and rivers of the Piddle and Winterborne. We climb the third highest hill in Dorset and are treated to views over north Dorset.

It is claimed that Puddletown was the inspiration for Weatherbury in Thomas Hardy's *Far from the Madding Crowd*. This route begins in a small lane called The Backwater beside the River Piddle. Heading east, we bear right, away from the river, then take the second left. The thatched cottage facing The Square was once home to Ralph Wightman (1901–71). Said to be Dorset's

first voice of radio, his dulcet tones were described as 'A sound like heather, honey and goose-grease'. The son of a local farmer, he was born in Piddletrenthide. In 1948 he became a full-time writer and broadcaster, and during WWII broadcast weekly 'Trans-Atlantic talks' to the United States on English country life.

At Troy House, which has two interesting stone heads on the end wall, we take the right fork past the church. Ahead, hidden behind other buildings, is impressive Ilsington House. The estate can be traced back to the 12th century and it was once owned (in 1724) by Robert Walpole, son of the country's first Prime Minister. One renowned tenant (between 1780

and 1830) was General Thomas Garth, principal squire to King George III, who is believed to have adopted the king's illegitimate grandson and raised him here.

This back road leads to Puddletown High Street, which was the original A35 before the bypass was built. We go left towards Athelhampton, whose magnificent House and Gardens are open to the public on Sundays to Thursdays, March to October. On Saturdays the venue is often used for weddings, and it has featured in films including *Sleuth* (1972, starring Sir Laurence Olivier and Michael Caine) and more recently the Julian Fellowes-directed film *From Time to Time* (with Maggie Smith and Dominic West).

After a couple of miles we reach Tolpuddle, home of the Tolpuddle Martyrs Museum, which tells the tale of their arrest, trial and transportation in 1834, all of which led indirectly to the foundation of modern-day trade unionism. Neil Kinnock spoke at the 150th Anniversary Rally in 1985. More recently, Jeremy Corbyn addressed crowds at the annual Tolpuddle Martyrs Festival and took part in a procession through the village. At the thatched memorial seat and martyrs' tree we turn right towards Southover, pausing to admire the Old Mill, Manor House and little bridge over the River Piddle.

In Affpuddle we go straight on to the main road, signposted Crossways. Here we can see East Farm House (formerly Affpuddle Manor) on our left. The Frampton family owned the manor during the 1830s and their testimony played a major part in convicting the martyrs. A labourer named John Lock who gave key evidence against the men also lived in Affpuddle. We carry straight on at a sharp bend, leaving the main road, and descend into Briantspuddle, which consisted of 12 cottages before being developed into a model village during the early 20th century by Sir Ernest Debenham (of department store fame). Intended as a self-sufficient agricultural enterprise, the venture was only partially successful, but its legacy is a thriving community. In 1918, Debenham commissioned sculptor Eric Gill to design a war memorial in situ using Portland stone. Gill was a controversial character, and in her 1989 biography, cultural historian Fiona MacCarthy depicts him as a man with unsavoury sexual appetites. However, his work was of high quality and Briantspuddle's war memorial is undeniably impressive.

At the crossroads we go straight ahead to reach Throop, where we leave the tarmacked road and take a track on the left towards Turners Puddle. *The track is a bridleway, so motorists must continue along the road to the right to a crossroads and turn left through Moreton plantation. If wishing to visit Holy Trinity Church, you should turn left at the other end of the no-through road and continue for about half a mile.* We push the tandem over a couple of footbridges that span the river, stopping to look for fish. When we were several decades

younger we used to cycle across the most robust of these bridges but now we are more cautious. I am, anyway. Holy Trinity Church dates back more than 500 years but was deconsecrated in 1974. It is no longer open to the public except for occasional concerts and exhibitions, such as those held during Dorset Art Weeks. According to the church guide, two bells were stolen in the 1950s, turning up eventually one Christmas Eve at the gates of the nearby farmhouse, covered in soil, with a brief note saying 'Sorry Xmas'.

Back on the tandem we cycle down the lane, past a scattering of pretty cottages that comprise the hamlet of Turners Puddle. We go left at the junction and up to the road, where we turn right, then after a short distance bear left signed Bere Heath. At the next crossroads we turn left again to follow a straight road ahead to Bloxworth. This is an area popular with skylarks and it's always a joy to hear their song again after winter. We reach a junction with a cycle path straight ahead, so we follow this to the A35. ***Motorists should turn left up to the A35, then right to rejoin the route.***

We go right onto the main road and after about 180 m turn left to Bloxworth. We used to sometimes hear the cuckoo along these lanes but not for many a year now. At a T-junction with a bus stop ahead we bear left and follow the road round to the right for about a mile before reaching another T-junction with a yew tree on the right. Here we turn left and soon reach the A31, where we need to take care crossing the road. On our left is perhaps the most well known of Dorset's four 'Red Posts'. Popular beliefs are that this signpost marked the route convicts followed from Dorchester prison to Portsmouth before transportation to Botany Bay in Australia; it might have acted as a

reference point for illiterate guards who were escorting the prisoners; or it could be the location of a gibbet, since convicts were frequently hanged if they became troublesome on route. Nearby Botany Bay Inne has a large exterior mural depicting Captain Cook's landing at Botany Bay in 1770, supporting the first theory.

We cycle through Winterborne Tomson, stopping to look in the secluded church of St Andrew, with its wooden-barrelled ceiling and box pews exclusively for the use of local gentry in years gone by; poor folk were obliged to stand at the back. In the early 20th century the church was sadly neglected and farm animals found shelter within its walls. It was saved from ruin in

1931 when the Society for the Protection of Ancient Buildings sold a collection of Thomas Hardy manuscripts to pay for repairs. There is no electricity and no regular services here, though Advent Sunday is celebrated every year, and very atmospheric it is too, with only shadowy candle light to identify each chilly but enchanted villager.

We proceed on past Anderson Manor, owned by Jeremy and Rosemary Isaac who have lived here for almost 40 years. The gardens are occasionally open to the public. During WWII this 16th-century manor was the operational base and training centre for the Small Scale Raiding Force (SSRF)–62 Commando. This Special Operations Executive-sponsored unit specialised in night-time raids across the Channel to snatch prisoners for interrogation, reconnoitre enemy installations and, on one occasion, capture and bring back to England the entire German crew of the Casquets lighthouse on Guernsey. The 55 members of the SSRF lived and trained at Anderson.

From here it's only a couple of miles to Winterborne Kingston. After paying our respects at the war memorial beside the village hall, we cycle along West Street, towards Winterborne Whitechurch. Not much more than a peaceful lane, there's little traffic apart from the occasional horse rider. Horses tend to be nervous of cyclists, so we approach slowly and Allan calls out a greeting when we draw close. 'Cyclist behind!' is his usual salutation, and then something along the lines of 'Nice day for it' as we pass by. This might sound odd but it generally allays any fears the horse might have and riders always smile, so we must be doing something right. I guess the last thing they want is a cyclist silently streaking up behind and whizzing by at about 20 mph.

After passing East Farm Shop, at the crossroads with the Milton Arms in front we turn right onto the A354 and then immediately left up Whatcombe Lane towards Winterborne Stickland. This is another quiet lane with a couple of interesting manor houses. Whatcombe House has a long narrow driveway through parkland, with a sign asking motorists not to exceed 30 mph. This amuses me because really that would be quite a nippy pace along there. Built in 1752, Whatcombe was family owned for many years. Possession of the house descended by marriage through the Mansells of Smedmore, and a nearby cottage is named Mansells. Whatcombe was taken over in 1960 by an international spiritual movement called Subud. Patrick Harding and Derek Inwood (both schoolmasters and members of Subud) established a residential school here for troubled teenage boys, many of whom came from London. In 1980 the house returned to private ownership.

In Winterborne Clenston, the attractive church of St Nicholas is perhaps best known for its impressive spire, a fairly unusual feature in Dorset. The seat in the churchyard has a design of oak leaves and the dedication reads 'Treasured memories of George Wallbridge. Lovingly donated by his wife

and family'. George and his wife Winifred bought a smallholding here, where they grew their own produce and brought up six children. A quiet couple, they sat at the back of the church, enjoying the old-fashioned services. George was very gentlemanly and always wore a bow tie. We sit and admire the gravestones.

We cycle on past Winterborne Clenston manor house, which has been in the same family for almost 800 years. Names have changed though because on several occasions the property has passed down the female line. At present it is owned by the Carlyle-Clarke family, whose lineage can be traced back to the *Domesday Book*.

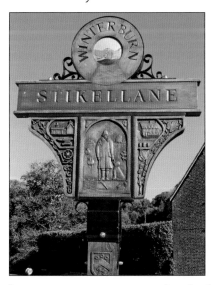

At Winterborne Stickland by the school we pass the village sign on our left. Unveiled in 1988 by the sculptress Dame Elizabeth Frink who lived in nearby Woolland, this portrays local industries such as brewing, spinning, button making and working the land. On one side the village's name is shown as Winterburn Stikellane, which is how it was known in the year 1203.

We fork left towards Winterborne Houghton, then left again at the church to head up the valley, with the stream our constant companion. We used to see an occasional water vole here and recently the odd flash of a kingfisher. I have my eye on a pretty thatched cottage but it's never been up for sale. A local woman named Loeta Hall began working part-time in the former post office in Houghton in 1915. Mrs Hall eventually retired in 1995 at the age of 93. Now that's dedication! At Houghton Springs Fish Farm, we meet George,

a worker on the farm. The fish are fed three to four times a day. They sell 150 kg of rainbow trout a week and it is the only place in Dorset that sells Arctic Char, which are shipped as far as Singapore.

In Houghton, after turning right towards Bulbarrow we begin the long climb. This hill always defeats us at the same point and we get off near some farm buildings where in spring we often linger to admire the lambs. Allan and I start cycling again when the incline becomes less challenging, but it's still puffy pedalling to the top for a few miles. At the T-junction we go left, then ignore the next left turn to Milton Abbas and go on towards Bulbarrow. In early spring the wooded area around here is a glorious sight, awash with British bluebells, quite different from the Spanish variety that has invaded our gardens and threatens to crossbreed with our native bluebell. These intruders are unscented, whereas British bluebells have a sweet, powerful fragrance. Wild garlic also thrives on the grass verges around here, so white flowers mingle with blue and spicy odours contend with sweet.

As we approach the staggered crossroads at Woolland Hill, named after the

village below the ridge, an amazing vista opens up to the right, looking north towards Sherborne and Yeovil. There is a large linear car park, and years ago there used to be an ice-cream van here on Sunday afternoons and we would look forward to a choc-ice on our rides.

We continue on, taking the right fork towards Stoke Wake. The tall aerial masts to our left stand on Bulbarrow Hill, at 274 m above sea level. TV presenter Jack Hargreaves, who died in 1994, asked for his ashes to be scattered here. We ignore the right turn to Woolland and continue about 600 m down the lane to visit Rawlsbury Camp, an Iron Age hillfort. We welcome the return of a wooden cross here, as there have been several versions over the years. The original oak cross was erected by Rev J.L. Baillie, vicar of Milborne St Andrew, with a little help from his friends, in readiness for an Open-Air Evensong service where 3,000 people congregated in torrential rain on 31 July 1966.

Returning to Bulbarrow Hill, we fork right just before the masts (there is confusion about which is Bulbarrow Hill and which is Woolland; Woolland Hill is often called Bulbarrow by locals). At the T-junction near the bottom of the hill is a memorial seat dedicated to four men who died in WWII. Here we turn right and then left, following the signs to The Fox and Lower Ansty. This is a complicated village, as there is also Higher Ansty and Little Ansty (aka Pleck).

We cycle past the 18th-century Fox Inn, which in the 1990s was renowned throughout Dorset as a destination pub. Even Allan and I went there occasionally, which is saying something. It became less popular but is on the up again. The phrase 'dog friendly' is used a lot these days, but this place really knows how to pamper your pooch. The Fox has a fully equipped dog wet room, with shower, grooming table, dryer, towels and shampoos. Opposite the pub is Brewery Farm Shop and Post Office, which stocks local produce.

In 1777, a Dorset farmer named Charles Hall founded the Ansty Brewery. The enterprise provided an abundance of local jobs including clerks, maltsters, coopers, barrel washers, pony boys and an engine driver who doubled as a rat catcher. At one time the company owned 20 horses and a number of carts and drays. It even had its own fire engine. Brewing ceased at Ansty in the 1940s, when the business now known as Hall & Woodhouse transferred to Blandford. The village hall used to be a brewery building, and the old malthouse became Malthouse Cottages. The stream that runs through the village, just below the old brewery buildings, is called Mash Water (the heated mixture of malted barley and water produced at the start of the brewing process is called 'mash').

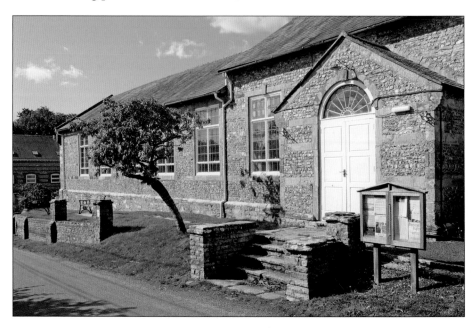

In 1976, Rev David Pennal revived the ancient tradition of Randy Day in Ansty. Young fellows armed with 3-ft-long bamboo poles decorated with streamers were cheered as they ran in hot pursuit of village maidens. The optimistic expectation was that girls prodded with poles would comply with the lads' amorous advances. Perhaps unsurprisingly, this initiative was not repeated and Randy Day once again lapsed into obscurity. The reverend also organised a wheelbarrow housebrick push, and was behind a record 121 people sitting in a circle on each other's knees with no other means of support. I have no idea what became of this unorthodox vicar.

We continue on through Melcombe Bingham, which is also known as Melcombe Horsey and, as if that isn't confusing enough, the manor house is a mile away and goes by the name of Bingham's Melcombe. Next is Cheselbourne, a small Dorset Downs village, and we pass the delightfully named Snails Creep and Old Chapel. The 14th-century St Martin's Church has a pinnacled tower with battlements and interesting canonical sundial.

Cheselbourne used to be the site of a tradition known as 'Treading in the Wheat', in which young women from the village dressed in white would walk the fields on Palm Sunday. There has been a school here since 1861 and girls and boys used to have separate entrances and playgrounds. Log Book extracts are interesting: for example, 9 July 1915: 'For the past few weeks attendance has been low because the boys have been at work on the farms. This seems to have been necessary as Cheselbourne has sent so many to war'; and 12 November 1918: 'Half Holiday granted because of the glorious news of peace'.

We turn right at the school towards Piddletrenthide and after some climbing are treated to great views across to Purbeck. At Thorncome Farm there is a bridleway sign on the right and a track to Lyscombe Farm, with a parking area and information sign about walks. We take this short detour to the beautifully situated 12th-century Lyscombe chapel, which after many uses had a Dutch Barn built over the ruins in 1957, and more recently underwent an award-winning restoration. The first service for 500 years was held in the chapel in 2007. The adjacent ruined cottage may not have

a protective roof, and has not fared so well, but is still very evocative, with its quirky features.

After visiting the chapel and back on the road, we pass the squeak and snuffle of Doles Ash Piggery before a steep descent to a T-junction in Piddletrenthide. Turning left we head south down the B3143 along the Piddle valley, through White Lackington and Piddlehinton. The area is well served with pubs – the Poachers Inn, Piddle Inn and Thimble Inn. There used to be another pub called the European, but that's now a private house. South House is a B&B and also a retreat for writers and artists, offering workshops throughout the year. Way's Forge in Piddlehinton dates back to the 1830s. This was a working forge run by five generations of the Way family and is now a holiday cottage. Just before Enterprise Park, fields to the right on either side of the track to Little Puddle Barn are the site of the medieval village of Little Piddle, and the bumps and ridges of earthworks stand out quite clearly. Maps show more earthworks further down this road, at the sharp right corner.

It's interesting that the modern settlements are further up the valley. Enterprise Park is home to Puddletown Rugby Club and Piddle Brewery. The quality of the local water is perhaps a factor for the latter.

Leaving the Piddle villages behind, we turn left towards Puddletown and follow the road past Waterston Manor, inspiration for Weatherbury Farm in Hardy's *Far From the Madding Crowd*. The wide driveway, lined with manicured yew bushes and lavender, passes through a gatehouse leading to the stone-built mansion, recorded in *Domesday Book* as a royal residence of King Harold and then William the Conqueror. The gardens are sometimes open to the public. On one such occasion, in June 2016, a Ming-style vase previously belonging to the Duke of Wellington was hidden in the 5 acres

of garden with clues to its whereabouts. Whoever found this treasure could keep it. After several hours searching, three children claimed their reward when they discovered the vase dangling on a piece of wire in the fishpond.

The roar of traffic seems very close towards the end of this road from the nearby dual carriageway, which we cycle over into Puddletown, reaching the Blue Vinny pub. The Davies family at Woodbridge Farm near Sturminster Newton is the only producer of the historic Blue Vinny cheese. Once made in almost every farmhouse in Dorset, production died out entirely during WWII. In the early 1980s, Michael Davies resurrected it using a 300-year-old recipe, and in 2018 it won Gold at the World Cheese Awards in Norway. The pub has a pretty garden, offering an ideal end to our tour.

# Route 9 – Moreton

*(visiting Tincleton, Bockhampton, West Stafford, Owermoigne, East Chaldon and Lulworth)*

**Distance:** 43 miles (70 km)

**Hills:** 370 m elevation change, four significant hills

**OS map:** Explorer 117 and OL15

**Brief description:** Through quiet lanes and villages we wend our way from Lawrence of Arabia's resting place to Thomas Hardy's birthplace. Lunch is on a bench above Lulworth Cove, with views of its white pebble beach, rock pools and towering cliffs. This is a tour of discoveries, not least two scenic castles, and of art, with sculptures, galleries and a church with Whistler-engraved windows.

From Moreton Tea Rooms we head west, but almost immediately bear right on Hurst Road (there is no signpost here). At the B3390 we turn right signed Affpuddle, cross two bridges over the River Frome and a tributary, passing a metal sculpture of two lovers and TWC (The Watercress Company), which owns several watercress farms in Dorset, Hampshire, Spain and Florida.

Taking the next left turn signed Dorchester, we follow the lane through the hamlet of Pallington past Sculpture by the Lakes. This is a 26-acre sculpture park created by Simon Gudgeon, one of Britain's leading contemporary sculptors, and his wife Monique. The dramatic outdoor works of art are set in peaceful gardens bordered by the river with three deep lakes. There is a café, but refreshingly visitors are invited to bring their own picnic.

A little further on, opposite Tincleton Lifestyle Centre, is the entrance to Clyffe House, quite obvious on the ridge to our right. Designed by Victorian architect Benjamin Ferrey and built in 1842, it replaced an older manor house which had been the birthplace of 17th-century lawyer and politician Clement Walker. Walker's open criticism of Oliver Cromwell led to his expulsion from Parliament in 1648 and imprisonment in the Tower of

London. A controversial character, he is thought to have terrorised his wife and forbade her speaking with friends unless he was present. At the church of St John the Evangelist we keep left. The Old School House on the right and church were also designed by Ferrey. The school is now Tincleton Gallery which exhibits contemporary fine art. We go straight on through Tincleton, to reach a staggered crossroads and head towards Dorchester.

Further on we ignore the right turn to Puddletown and Rhododendron Mile. In June this used to be a swathe of pink Rhododendron through the heart of Puddletown Forest, but much has been cut down. Continuing along our quiet lane we reach a crossroads. To the right is signed Hardy's Cottage, where the Dorset writer was born in 1840 and lived until his mid-30s. The cottage is owned by the National Trust and there is a café, toilets and Visitor Centre. Surrounding Thorncombe Woods offers pleasant walks at any time of year.

We turn left to Lower Bockhampton. The building that is Yalbury Cottage hotel and restaurant dates back around 350 years and was once the home of the local shepherd and the keeper of the water meadows. A little further down is the Old School House, hidden behind a hedge but discreetly viewable up Knapwater Lane. This is where young Hardy would have learned his times tables, but the school closed in 1961. Out of the village we cross several bridges over the River Frome, the first with an old deportation warning sign.

At the next T-junction we turn left to West Stafford and are now on NCN Route 2. We pass Stafford House, owned by Lord Julian Kitchener-Fellowes, award-winning actor, novelist, film director and screenwriter (his work includes *Downton Abbey*) and Conservative peer of the House of Lords. We bear left around the church and at the thatched shelter on the right is an informative sign about the village's history. For 100 years, prior to 1938, the Wise Man Inn had been the village shop and post office. It was destroyed by fire in 2006 and re-opened after a two-year restoration and rebuild. We continue past the pretty village hall and out of West Stafford. On our right is Talbothays Lodge, designed by Thomas Hardy for his brother and two sisters. As a young man, the author trained as an architect. Mary, Henry and Kate (his siblings) lived here until Mary's death in 1915. In Hardy's novels, West Stafford is known as Talbothays.

At the T-junction we turn left, then almost immediately left again past Lewell Barn. There is no road sign but the NCN sign points to Moreton. About a mile along this lane we arrive at Woodsford Castle and admire its splendid thatched roof. It was built in the 14th century, and at the age of 16, Hardy

assisted his father with architectural drawings for its restoration. The young Hardy impressed the owner, architect James Hicks, so much that he took him on as an apprentice. The house is now owned by the Landmark Trust and available as a holiday let.

After passing the church hidden behind thick foliage, and School Lane opposite, with its Old School House, we bear right near some tall pine trees. After about 300 m we turn right towards Crossways (this road isn't signed but there is a large open barn on the right). While we're consulting the map an elderly cyclist stops for a chat. It turns out that in the 1980s we'd all belonged to the Wessex Road Club, so we were soon catching up on news about riders we'd not seen for ages. Sadly, our informant knew of several deaths and it all began getting a bit melancholy, until he noticed Allan's Mont Ventoux cycling cap and that provided a welcome change of subject. He told us that he too had once tackled this Tour de France climb and ruefully admitted being overtaken by women!

It's a useful encounter because he gives us some helpful directions. We go over a level crossing into Crossways. At a crossroads we continue ahead up Woodsford Road, then at a T-junction turn right onto Paul's Way and almost immediately left onto Dick o'th Banks Road. After the sports fields and pavilion we come to a five-way crossing. Of the two roads opposite we take the one on the right, Moreton Road, signed Owermoigne.

We enjoy a pleasant swoop down through Moigne Combe Woods, looking out for the bulls that a sign says are for sale, before the road begins to open

up near Mill House Cider Museum. A 10-minute video shows how cider was made on 18th- and 19th-century equipment and you can bring your own apples for pressing. Tastings are available of the different ciders for sale in the shop. The Dorset Collection of Clocks is also housed here, with more than 30 Grandfather clocks.

Cycling into Owermoigne we pass the entrance to Moigne Court on our left. This manor house was built in 1267 and is the oldest inhabited house in Dorset, where eight generations of the Cree family have lived. It's surrounded by a rectangular moat and in its grounds are remains of a medieval fishpond. They run an interesting range of courses such as art, drama and meditation, and have wild camping and alternative accommodation for hire including a Vintage Bedford Lorry called 'The Homely Horsebox' and a converted 1971 coach, the 'Magic Bus'.

We continue into the village with the stream on our left and stop at a bench by St Michael's Church. This is a peaceful spot in the older part of Owermoigne, with some attractive thatched cottages. A notice tells us that the village participates in the Living Churchyard Project, a DWT initiative that since the 1990s has involved more than a hundred parishes. Ways in which churchyards can encourage wildlife include developing small areas of previously mown grass into mini wildflower meadows, replacing exotic shrubs with native species and planting nectar-rich flowers to encourage insects. There is a pleasant bench in a secluded snippet of woodland set aside for wildlife, called 'God's Pocket'. Owermoigne was involved in the 18th-century smuggling trade and St Michael's has a shady history. Barrels of brandy were stored in the church tower and the 16th-century Old Rectory near the end of Church Lane has a blocked-up window, through which the vicar's share was delivered. The wooden structure of the original house is formed from timbers of a Spanish Armada galleon wrecked at Ringstead Bay 3 miles away. Ironically, Owermoigne has never had a pub.

We continue on through the village to the main A352, where we turn left, passing a garage and Kate's Farm Shop, and continue for about half a mile, ignoring the right turn to Wyevale Garden Centre. Ours is the next right signed West Chaldon, and a steep climb awaits, made more arduous by a strong head wind. At the top of the hill Allan spots a crouched hare in an adjacent field, which obligingly leapt to its feet and sped away from us.

We soon leave the scattering of houses and farms that comprise West Chaldon and continue into Chaldon Herring (East Chaldon), passing Beth Car, where writer Theodore Powys once lived. In the 1920s and 1930s the village buzzed with creative folk. Writer Sylvia Townsend Warner lived here with poet Valentine Ackland and the two women are buried in St Nicholas' churchyard, as is sculptor Elizabeth Muntz. Llewellyn Powys also had a house

in the village. He was rumoured to have a penchant for lying naked on nearby cliffs on moonlit nights, and a headstone where his ashes were scattered can be found there. In front of the church is the village hall, built in 1847 by the Diocese of Salisbury to be a school for the 'poor persons of and in the Parish of Chaldon'. The old school bell is still in situ.

Continuing, we pass Apple Tree Cottage where Elizabeth Muntz lived. Probably her most unusual sculpture was based on a cat named Simon. He was the mascot of Royal Navy sloop the *Amethyst*. In 1949, while deployed on the Yangtze River, the ship was struck by bombs dropped by Chinese Communists. Simon was wounded but survived and remained on active service, raising morale and seeing off rats. He was given the Dickin Medal

for 'gallantry under fire' by the PDSA (People's Dispensary for Sick Animals), the highest award any animal can receive while serving in military conflict.

At the village green we bear right. To our left is the ford and it's the first time we've seen water flowing over it. The Sailor's Return pub is just up the hill beyond the ford. The name originates from the story of a sailor who, returning home, found his wife in the arms of a lover. Initially a pair of thatched cottages, it became an inn during the mid-19th century. Writer David Garnett, who used to visit the Sailor's Return, wrote a book of the same name in 1925.

Cycling out of the village we pass a lovely old barn with front arches held up on metal props. Then we follow close by the River Win to reach Winfrith Newburgh. At St Christopher's Church we turn right, signed West Lulworth. It's a steady climb to the entrance to Durdle Door Caravan Park, where motorists can park and walk down the steep cliff to the stone arch, one of the Jurassic Coast's most photographed landmarks. We continue left and are treated to splendid views of the sea and hills around Lulworth.

We freewheel down to the Cove, where we push the bike part way up the cliff to our favourite bench with great views of the white pebble beach, calm sea and towering cliffs surrounding this beautiful bay. There is a shortage of seats around here, so we are fortunate to find it unoccupied. The Cove is popular with tourists and there is ample parking, a visitor centre with toilets, places to eat and plenty of ice-cream opportunities.

After our picnic we backtrack through the village and go straight on towards Wool, passing the thatched Castle Inn. This dates from the 16th century and down the years has been called the Green Man, Travellers' Rest and Jolly Sailor. When the telephone was a luxury only wealthy people could afford, this pub had one of the few in West Lulworth and most villagers used it at some time or another.

A long steep hill comes next, and after a bit of a slog we pass Lulworth Camp near the summit. This British Army base was established in 1918 and is home to the Armoured Fighting Vehicle Gunnery School and Lulworth Ranges. There are some beautiful walks in the area with fantastic coastal views, but obviously the public is only allowed access when the Ranges are not in operation – access includes every day during summer and most (but not all) weekends throughout the year.

We turn right, signed East Lulworth, where you can often see (and hear) the army vehicles actually firing. On a little further we pass Lulworth Castle, for centuries home of the Weld family, current owners of Lulworth Estate. Built in 1588 as a hunting lodge to entertain aristocracy and royalty, it was destroyed by fire in 1929. Partly restored, the castle is usually open on Sundays–Fridays; it's also a wedding venue and hosts the annual music festival Camp Bestival. There are several walks around the park including one to the lake, which is our favourite. Leaflets about these walks can be purchased at the Castle.

Bearing left past the Castle into East Lulworth, we see the thatched Weld Arms. In 2007 an unexploded WWII bomb was found beneath the beer garden, where customers sat in blissful ignorance for years. Next is Cockles

Lane and the Old School, now Past & Presents Gift Shop and Tea Rooms. I can thoroughly recommend the lemon tart! On the next right bend opposite the exit from the Castle grounds is a memorial to the villagers lost during WWI.

*If the Ranges, and therefore the roads east, happen to be closed, just take the left turn north towards Coombe Keynes, then turn right and pick up the route at Wool.*

If the Ranges are open, take the road opposite the entrance to Lulworth Castle, then take the right fork and climb up past Whiteway Hill, Povington Hill and West Creech Hill. At the top you will be treated to splendid sea views, particularly if you make the 2-km walk west along the ridge to Flower's Barrow, and its Iron Age hillfort earthworks. You can also look down over deserted Tyneham village, which was evacuated in December 1943 due to WWII, and is now a museum of sorts. Its properties are mainly ruins, but the exhibitions in the church and school, and the information boards are all fascinating. We ignore the right turn down to Tyneham this time, and continue atop the ridge – one of our favourite roads to cycle. We exit the Ranges, and at the T-junction go left (straight on really) and enjoy the 20% (1 in 5) descent of Grange Hill. At the bottom, we ignore all the turnings around Grange Farm, and after about 2 km, opposite the Springfield Hotel, turn left towards East Holme, again on NCN Route 2.

This is a pretty but rather dark, tree-covered lane. We ignore the right turn to East Holme and about 1 km further on we reach West Holme crossroads. To the right is Holme for Gardens, with its popular tearooms,

but we go straight across towards East Stoke. After 1 mile we ignore the next crossroads to East Stoke and continue on towards Wool. After skirting Bindon Farm, we pass Bindon Abbey House Wellness Retreat and Bindon Mill alongside the River Frome (both private). A Cistercian monastery was built here in 1172, and its foundations, some church walls, gardens and moated areas can still be seen. Apparently, stone from the abbey was used to build Lulworth Castle.

The last stretch into Wool has the London Waterloo–Weymouth railway line to our right. We've not lacked refreshment opportunities today, but should you need more, just left at the T-junction is the Black Bear pub and a well-stocked Spar store. There's also Williams the Baker, where three generations of Williams have been bakers since 1928. All production takes place here, including 20 different flavoured flapjack bars, after they took over the Dorset Flapjack Company in 2009; these are distributed around the country and to Spain, Switzerland, the Netherlands, Germany and the Canary Islands.

However, we turn right past the railway station and right again over the level-crossing. We take a slight detour to see Woolbridge Manor on the banks of the River Frome and beside the 16th-century Wool Bridge, considered to be the best-preserved Elizabethan bridge in Dorset. Due to damage caused by movement of tanks in both World Wars it has been closed to traffic for many years and is only accessible on foot or by bicycle. The nearby manor house was built in the 12th century. It belonged to the Abbey of Bindon, then

to the Dorset Turberville family, after which it was sold to Henry Drax of Charborough Park. Close to the bridge is an informative sign about nearby Bovington Garrison, home of the Army's tanks and armoured fighting vehicles since 1916.

Backtracking slightly, we take the right turn immediately before the railway line signed Moreton. Pedalling through East Burton we notice a cast-iron sign on a garden gate: 'Penalty for not shutting the gate £2'. This probably originated at a pedestrian railway crossing. We pass a signpost for the intriguingly named hamlet Giddy Green, and carry on past the Seven Stars pub. The original Seven Stars burnt down in 1928 and was rebuilt 10 years later with a thatched roof, which was probably asking for trouble. Sure enough, this too was destroyed by flames and rebuilt in its present form.

After a while we pass the back of Winfrith Atomic Energy Establishment. The site opened in 1958 and there used to be nine experimental reactors here. Pioneering research was carried out in the 1960s and 1970s, giving employment to over 2000 people. In 1990 the government decided Winfrith had served its purpose and plans were drawn up for decommissioning, with the final reactor core to be removed by 2020. Work is now focused on returning part of the site to heathland, including infilling a 1-million gallon water tank under Blacknoll Hill. When complete, Winfrith will be the first nuclear site in the UK to be fully decommissioned. However, there is still a licence for radioactive waste treatment and recycling. The site was given Enterprise Zone status in 2017, and as Dorset Innovation Park is developing 'an advanced engineering cluster of excellence in the South West, building on strengths in marine, defence and energy'.

Over Broomhill bridge and around the corner we soon see Moreton House on our right, offering upmarket holiday accommodation. It was built in 1744 for the Frampton family, who have owned the estate for about 600 years. Looking back, there is an obelisk on Fir Hill, erected in 1786 as a memorial to James Frampton.

On into Moreton, and next to the Walled Garden we stop to visit the grave of T.E. Lawrence, better known as Lawrence of Arabia. I have vivid memories of seeing the film back in 1963, when as a 13-year-old girl I fell completely in love with Peter O'Toole. The cemetery porch comprises an unusual lych-gate, originally positioned at the entrance to the kitchen gardens of Moreton House. Lych-gates were meeting places and shelters for people bringing a body for burial and where the priest received the corpse. The 1549 prayer book required the priest to meet bearers of the corpse at the churchyard entrance, so lych-gates provided shelter from bad weather for mourners.

Lawrence lived a couple of miles away across the heath at Clouds Hill. A letter to Nancy Astor (first female Member of Parliament) reveals his fondness for his little cottage: 'Wild mares would not at present take me away from Clouds Hill. It is an earthly paradise and I am staying here until I feel qualified for it.' Strangely, the great man's headstone fails to mention his exploits in Arabia, where he led the Arab revolt against the Turks during WWI. It only records his connection with Oxford University, where he gained a first-class degree in history, with an open book at the foot of the grave displaying the university's motto *Dominus Illuminatio Mea* (The Lord is my Light). A keen motorcyclist, Lawrence was riding his Brough Superior SS100 when he crashed near Moreton in 1935. It is thought he swerved to avoid two children on bicycles. He never regained consciousness and died in the military hospital at Bovington Camp 6 days later. The neurosurgeon who attended him (Hugh Cairns) began work on research that led to the use of crash helmets by both military and civilian motorcyclists.

We linger in the cemetery, before paying a visit to the Tea Rooms, in what was the old school house. School photographs on the walls date back to the 1920s. There are also photographs of Lawrence and copies of letters he exchanged with friends. The 'bier' cart that carried his coffin now serves as a trolley for cakes and scones.

The sun is shining and we are enjoying our brief sojourn from cycling, so we wander down the lane to the right of the Tea Rooms. St Nicholas Church is particularly worth a visit because of its beautiful window engravings by Laurence Whistler. Lawrence's funeral took place here in May 1935. It was a simple service, but the host of eminent mourners included WWI poet Siegfried Sassoon, Nancy Astor and Winston Churchill. The village school provided the choir and among its number were the twins Walter and Harry Pitman who refuelled Lawrence's motorbike at Bovington immediately before the accident. Further down the lane we pass the Grade II Listed building that used to be the village store and post office. At the ford a footbridge spans a wide stretch of the River Frome. This is a popular place with children and dogs paddling in the shallow water. The bridge leads to several short forest walks, as well as a bridleway to Clouds Hill (National Trust).

# About the Author

Jackie Winter was born in Dorset and has lived in Winterborne Zelston, near Blandford, since 1981. She spent her working life in Dorset County Libraries, and in 2016 published *Lipsticks and Library Books: The Story of Boots Booklovers Library.* She has always enjoyed writing (short stories, articles and books) and has been successful in several writing competitions, once winning first prize of £1000. She has cycled the Dorset lanes with her husband Allan for more than 40 years and in 2014 published *Life in Tandem: Tales of Cycling Travels.* It would be fair to say that if she's not out cycling, she's probably writing about it.

# Some other books by Roving Press

If you enjoyed this book, why not try others in our range of local titles?

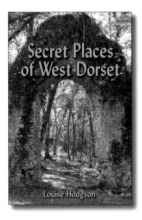

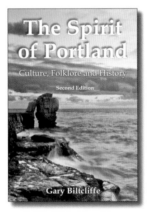

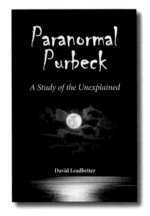

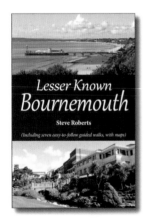

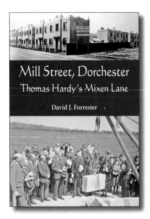

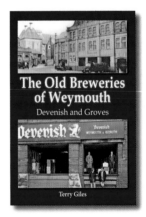

www.rovingpress.co.uk

*If you like exploring, you'll love our books*